双双中文教材（17）
Chinese Language and Culture Course

中文科普阅读 Chinese Reading of Popular Science

王双双 编著

北京大学出版社
PEKING UNIVERSITY PRESS

图书在版编目（CIP）数据

中文科普阅读/王双双 编著．—北京：北京大学出版社，2007.7
（双双中文教材17）
ISBN 978-7-301-08711-4

Ⅰ．中… Ⅱ．王… Ⅲ．汉语–对外汉语教学–教材 Ⅳ．H195.4

中国版本图书馆CIP数据核字（2005）第075449号

书　　　名：	中文科普阅读
著作责任者：	王双双　编著
英　文翻　译：	王亦兵
责　任编　辑：	邓晓霞　dxxvip@vip.sina.com
标　准书　号：	ISBN 978-7-301-08711-4/H·1447
出　版发　行：	北京大学出版社
地　　　址：	北京市海淀区成府路205号 100871
网　　　址：	http://www.pup.cn
电　　　话：	邮购部 62752015　发行部 62750672　编辑部 62752028　出版部 62754962
电　子信　箱：	zpup@pup.pku.edu.cn
印　　刷　者：	北京大学印刷厂
经　　销　者：	新华书店
	889毫米×1194毫米　16开本　11印张　196千字
	2007年7月第1版　2016年3月第3次印刷
定　　　价：	65.00元

未经许可，不得以任何方式复制或抄袭本书之部分或全部内容。
版权所有，侵权必究
举报电话：（010）62752024
电子信箱：fd@pup.pku.edu.cn

前言

《双双中文教材》是一套专门为海外青少年编写的中文课本，是我在美国八年的中文教学实践基础上编写成的。在介绍这套教材之前，请读一首小诗：

> 一双神奇的手，
> 推开一扇窗。
> 一条神奇的路，
> 通向灿烂的中华文化。
>
> 鲍凯文 鲍维江
> 1998年

鲍维江和鲍凯文姐弟俩是美国生美国长的孩子，也是我的学生。1998年冬，他们送给我的新年贺卡上的小诗，深深地打动了我的心。我把这首诗看成我文化教学的"回声"。我要传达给海外每位中文老师：我教给他们（学生）中国文化，他们思考了、接受了、回应了。这条路走通了！

语言是交际的工具，更是一种文化和一种生活方式，所以学习中文也就离不开中华文化的学习。汉字是一种古老的象形文字，她从远古走来，带有大量的文化信息，但学起来并不容易。使学生增强兴趣、减小难度，走出苦学汉字的怪圈，走进领悟中华文化的花园，是我编写这套教材的初衷。

学生不论大小，天生都有求知的欲望，都有欣赏文化美的追求。中华文化本身是魅力十足的。把这宏大而玄妙的文化，深入浅出地，有声有色地介绍出来，让这迷人的文化如涓涓细流，一点一滴地渗入学生们的心田，使学生们逐步体味中国文化，是我编写这套教材的目的。

为此我将汉字的学习放入文化介绍的流程之中同步进行，让同学们在学中国地理的同时，学习汉字；在学中国历史的同时，学习汉字；在学中国哲学的同时，学习汉字；在学中国科普文选的同时，学习汉字……

这样的一种中文学习，知识性强，趣味性强；老师易教，学生易学。当学生们合上书本时，他们的眼前是中国的大好河山，是中国五千年的历史和妙不可言的哲学思维，是奔腾的现代中国……

总之，他们了解了中华文化，就会探索这片土地，热爱这片土地，就会与中国结下情缘。

最后我要衷心地感谢所有热情支持和帮助我编写教材的老师、家长、学生、朋友和家人，特别是老同学唐玲教授、何茜老师、我姐姐王欣欣编审及我女儿Uta Guo年复一年的鼎力相助。可以说这套教材是大家努力的结果。

王双双
2005年5月8日

说明

《双双中文教材》是一套专门为海外学生编写的中文教材。它是由美国加州王双双老师和中国专家学者共同努力,在海外多年的实践中编写出来的。全书共20册,识字量2500个,包括了从识字、拼音、句型、短文的学习,到初步的较系统的中国文化的学习。教材大体介绍了中国地理、历史、哲学等方面的丰富内容,突出了中国文化的魅力。课本知识面广,趣味性强,深入浅出,易教易学。

这套教材体系完整、构架灵活、使用面广。学生可以从零起点开始,一直学完全部课程20册;也可以将后11册(10～20册)的九个文化专题和第五册(汉语拼音)单独使用,这样便于高中和大学开设中国哲学、地理、历史等专门课程以及假期班、短期中国文化班、拼音速成班使用,符合了美国AP中文课程的目标和基本要求。

本书是《双双中文教材》的第十七册,适用于已学习、掌握1200个以上汉字的学生使用。

本册讲的是科普知识,主要介绍了中国特有的自然科学知识。课文知识面广、趣味性强,语言比较简单。通过对本书的学习,学生们不仅能掌握一些科技词汇,而且能增进对中国的自然风貌、人文历史的了解,为今后阅读中文书报打下良好的基础。同时,学生们也能进一步增强环境保护的意识,达到既学中文又学科技的双重目的。

课文大多是根据一些优秀的中国科普读物加工、改编而成的,一般都注明了出处。但也有的课文是在综合了多个资料的基础上重新编写出来的。根据惯例,这样的课文就不加注了。

编者

课程设置

一年级	中文课本(第一册)	中文课本(第二册)	中文课本(第三册)
二年级	中文课本(第四册)	中文课本(第五册)	中文课本(第六册)
三年级	中文课本(第七册)	中文课本(第八册)	中文课本(第九册)
四年级	中国成语故事	中国地理常识	
五年级	中国古代故事	中国神话传说	
六年级	中国古代科学技术	中国文学欣赏	
七年级	中国诗歌欣赏	中文科普阅读	
八年级	中国古代哲学	中国历史(上)	
九年级	中国历史(下)	小说阅读，中文 SAT II	
十年级	中文 SAT II (强化班)	小说阅读，中文 SAT II 考试	

目录

第一课	黄河的源头（一）	1
第二课	黄河的源头（二）	10
第三课	银杏和水杉	19
第四课	跳伞	28
第五课	野骆驼	38
第六课	恒星真的不动吗？	49
第七课	灰尘的旅行	57
第八课	盐井和井盐	68
第九课	我们应该长多高	80
第十课	沙漠	90
生字表		103
生词表		105

第一课

黄河的源头（一）

人们打开一幅中国地图，就会看到一条弯弯曲曲的大河，像巨龙似的横卧在中国北方大地上。

黄河——中国的第二大河，全长5464千米，从河源到河口，要是坐上每小时50千米的火车，也要不停地跑上5天5夜。黄河不仅是中国的一条巨川，也是世界上一条著名的大河。

唐代诗人李白曾在诗中写道："黄河之水天上来，奔流到海不复回。"这当然只是诗歌，黄河水是不会从天上来的。那么，黄河水究竟是从哪里来的？这可是一个经过多少年才弄清楚的问题。

2000多年前，汉朝的张骞(qiān)出使西域回来后，向汉武帝报告："在西域时，听人说黄河水是从塔里木河流来的。"他认为这不大可能，因为他已经知道塔里木河是流入罗布泊的。直到晋朝，张华在他的《博物志》中才提出比较正确的观点，认为黄河发源于"星宿(xiù)海"，可是谁也不能证实他的说法对不对。

公元1280年，元朝政府为了找黄河源，派出了第一个河源考察队，进入青海地区的高原。在茫茫的高原上，他们寻找了四个多月，走到星宿海后，又沿着一条从西南方向流入星宿海的小河走了一百多里，但是，没有再继续找寻下去。在这次考察中，他们对星宿海地区作了许多珍贵的记录，使人们第一次知道了这个边远地带的详细情况，可惜的是，他们画的地图没有流传下来。此后，人们只知道黄河源在星宿海某地，对"河出星宿"之说有了较深的认识。

四百多年后的 1704 年，清朝的康熙(xī)皇帝又派出考察队进入青海，再次寻找黄河源，但也只是走到星宿海就再没有前进了。

公元 1782 年，清朝乾(qián)隆皇帝派人继续去寻找黄河源头。这一次，他们开始走出星宿海去寻找。他们在星宿海西南不远的地方发现一条黄色的河流，河口西面有一块大岩石，岩石上有一个终年不断涌水的喷泉。他们认为这一股清亮的泉水一定是黄河的源头了。他们称这条河流为"阿勒坦郭勒"（蒙语"黄金河"）。回到北京以后，他们向皇帝报告说，黄河发源地就在阿勒坦郭勒那里。但是根据他们所说的方位和情况，这条河应该是卡日曲。这就引起了后世关于黄河正源到底是哪条河的争议。

1952 年，中国又派出一支由 60 多人组成的河源考察队，开始在青海南部的高原上仔细地查找每一条可能是黄河源头的河流。队员们穿过千里无人的草原，越过高山，四个多月走了 5000

多千米的路程，到了星宿海后，看见一条从西边流过来的河流，很像是黄河源头的一部分。队员们沿着这条河，一直走进了约古宗列盆地。这个盆地面积约300平方千米，很久以前，曾是一个大湖泊，后来，由于气候的变化，湖水一天天少了。到现在剩下的湖水，分成了170多个小湖泊，散(sàn)布在原来的湖底上。河水像一条带子弯弯曲曲地从盆地中间流过。过了约古宗列盆地后，河床越来越窄了，到达源头时，河宽不到两米了。考察队员发现在河流尽头，有一个面积约三四平方米的小泉，像开水似的，翻滚起伏，泉柱发出非常好听的"叮叮咚咚"的声音。考察队员们高兴极了！他们一口气跑上小泉西边的山头，兴奋地向四周远望：一座高大的雪山——巴颜喀(kā)拉山的主峰雅拉达泽（海拔5442米），屹立在小泉的西边，好像一位士兵守卫在那里。考察队认为他们找到的这条河（约古宗列曲）就是黄河的正源。他们在这里立了一块高大的石碑，上面刻着"黄河源"三个大字和一行藏文。

可是，1978年青

海省又组织了一次考察，认定卡日曲是黄河的正源。后来人们从卫星照片上也发现，从南边汇入黄河的卡日曲比约古宗列曲还长25千米。根据"河源唯远"的原则，从长度来看，南源卡日曲应该是黄河的正源。几千年来的黄河源之谜终于弄清楚了。

有趣的是，黄河南源卡日曲与长江源头通天河的支流只隔着一道低矮的山岭，相距只有200米左右。这一对几乎从同一个地区流出的"姐妹河"在青海南部的高原上挥手告别之后，一个流过中国南方大地，一个流过中国北方大地。

（根据罗枢运、赵合顺《奔腾的黄河》改编）

生词

jiū jìng	究竟	on earth	dīng dōng	叮咚	tinkle
zhèng shí	证实	verify	yǎ lā dá zé	雅拉达泽	a name of a mountain
kǎo chá	考察	make an on-the-spot investigation	yì lì	屹立	stand; erect
mǒu	某	some; a certain	shí bēi	石碑	stone tablet
pēn quán	喷泉	fountain	yuán zé	原则	principle
tǎn	坦	even; a character of a river name	mí yǔ	谜（语）	riddle
lù chéng	路程	journey	huī shǒu	挥手	wave one's hand
zōng	宗	ancestor; a character of a river name;		

听写

究竟　某个　路程　喷泉　始终　谜　兴奋　挥手

宗　证实　*屹立　石碑

注：*以后为选做题，后同。

比一比

$$横\begin{cases}横穿\\横卧\\横线\end{cases} \quad 曲\begin{cases}弯曲\\乐曲\\歌曲\end{cases} \quad 兴\begin{cases}兴奋\\高兴\\兴趣\end{cases}$$

$$程\begin{cases}路程\\课程\end{cases} \quad 究\begin{cases}究竟\\研究\end{cases} \quad 喷\begin{cases}喷泉\\喷水\end{cases}$$

$$\begin{cases}玛（玛曲）\\妈（妈妈）\end{cases} \quad \begin{cases}迷（迷路）\\谜（谜语）\end{cases} \quad \begin{cases}屹（屹立）\\吃（吃饭）\end{cases}$$

字词运用

弯曲　乐曲　歌曲

一条小路弯弯曲曲通向远方。

他在音乐会上演奏了一首中国民间乐曲。

这是一首儿童歌曲。

究竟

黄河水究竟是从哪里来的？

明天的舞会你究竟去不去？

博物馆　博士

我在北京参观了历史博物馆和自然博物馆。

小辉的哥哥是医学博士。

反义词

弯曲——笔直　　　宽——窄　　　揭开——贴上

正确——错误　　　横——竖

词语解释

终年——从年头到年尾。

告别——离别、分手。

阅读

天鹅湖

中国的"天鹅湖"位于新疆巴音布鲁克草原上。它是一座高山湖泊，四周是天山的冰峰。巴音布鲁克天鹅湖东西长30千米，南北宽10千米，湖泊四周有许多清泉。春天，融化的雪水流入湖中。湖水清澈宁静，湖边绿草如茵。在遥远的印度和非洲南部过冬的天鹅，每到春季，都会飞回这里繁殖后代。这时，湖上的天鹅成千上万：它们有的在湖中漫游玩耍，有的在湖边草丛里做窝生蛋，有的飞翔在蓝天白云之间……那些小天鹅出壳三四个小时就能和爸爸妈妈一样，跑到湖中去游水寻找食物。小天鹅长得很快，只要三个月，便可长到10公斤重。

巴音布鲁克天鹅湖是目前世界上天鹅最集中的地区之一。为了保护这里的天鹅，1986年，中国在这里建立了自然保护区。

巴音布鲁克湖

Lesson One

The Source of the Yellow River (I)

When you look at a map of China, you will see a winding river spanning northern China like a gigantic dragon.

The Yellow River is the second longest river in China with a total length of 5,464 kilometers. It takes five consecutive days and nights by train at the speed of 50 kilometers per hour traveling from its riverhead to river mouth. It is an important river in China and one of the most famous rivers in the world.

Li Bai, a great poet of the Tang Dynasty, once praised the river in his poem: "Do you not see the Yellow River coming from the sky, Rushing into the sea and never come back?" But a poem is creative writing and it is impossible for a river to originate from the sky. Where on earth is the source of this great river? This is a question whose answer becomes clear after many, many years of exploration.

In the Han Dynasty, more than 2,000 years ago, Zhang Qian went to the Western Regions as a diplomatic envoy and reported on his return to the Emperor Han Wudi: "When I was in the Western Regions, I heard that the Yellow River originated from the Tarim River." But he believed that this was probably not the case, for he already knew that the Tarim River flew into the Lop Nur Lake. Then in the Jin Dynasty, Zhang Hua recorded a closer answer of the Star Sea in his *Bowu Zhi*: *Treatise on Curiosities*. But at that time, nobody could verify his conclusion.

In 1280 during the Yuan Dynasty, the government sent the firs expedition team to locate the source of the Yellow River. They went to the Qinghai Plateau and spent more than four months there searching for it. They once reached the Star Sea, yet then followed a small river flowing into the Star Sea from southwest and traced it for more than one hundred li (50 kilometers) before giving up. During the expedition, they left many precious records about the area around the Star Sea, allowing people to understand the details of this remote area for the first time. But it's a pity the map they drew got lost and people only knew that the river originated from somewhere around the Star Sea yet at the same time also had a better understanding about its origin.

More than 400 years later and in 1704 during the Qing Dynasty, the Emperor Kangxi sent another expedition team into Qinghai to continue the task of finding the source of the Yellow River. But again, they stopped at the Star Sea and didn't go any further from there.

In 1782 during the Qing Dynasty, the Emperor Qianlong once again sent an expedition team to look for the source and this time, they cast their eyes beyond the Star Sea. To the southwest of the Star Sea, they found to the west of the river mouth a large rock with a spring that flew all year round. They believed that this spring must be the origin of the Yellow River and named it Ahletan-guole (meaning the River of Gold in Mongolian). They reported to the emperor on returning to Beijing that the origin of the Yellow River was Ahletan-guole. But according to their recorded location and description, the river should be the Karequ river and their conclusion initiated the controversy about the real source of the Yellow River.

In 1952, Chinese government sent an expedition team composed of more than 60 members to examine each river on the Qinghai Plateau that was the possible source. The team traveled more than 5,000 kilometers in four months through unmanned plain and mountain. At arriving at the Star Sea, they noticed a river flow westward to the sea. The team suspected that it was part of the source they were looking for. So they walked along the river and entered the Yueguzonglie Basin (literally meaning a pot for stirring-frying highland barley in Tibetan). The total area of the basin is about 300 square kilometers and it used to be a large lake a long time ago. Then the lake shrank gradually due to the change of climate and formed more than 170 small lakes scattered on the original lake floor. The river winded through the basin center like a shining ribbon and narrowed gradually after it passed through the basin down to no more than two meters wide at its source. The expeditioners found a small spring of three or four square meters at the end of the river; the spring rose and fell like boiling water, producing pleasant tinkling sound. The expeditioners were overjoyed and ran to the top of the hill west to the spring, examining the surrounding landform. The Yaladaze Peak (5,442 meters high above sea level) of the lofty snow mountain Bayankala Mountain (also know as the Bayan Har Mountain, meaning rich black mountain in Mongolian) is located to the west of the small spring, guarding the origin of the Yellow River. The expedition team believed that the river (the Yueguzonglie River) was the real source of the great river. They erected a high stone table with three big characters-Huanghe Yuan (the soarce of the Yellow River) and a line of Tibetan words.

But later on and in 1978, Qinghai Province organized an expedition and believed that the real source should be the Karequ River. Later, people discovered from the satellite photographes that Karequ to the south of Maqu was 25 km longer than Yueguzonglie. Since the basic principle of deciding the river source is that "the length of a river counts", therefore, the south source of Karequ should be the real origin of the Yellow River. The mystery of the Yellow River source has finally been solved.

There is a fascinating fact: the distance between Karequ, the south source of the Yellow River, and a branch of the Tongtian River, the upper source of the Changjiang River, is only 200 meters and they are separated from each other by a low mountain range. The two Sister Rivers originate from the same area, part on the Qinghai Plateau and start their different journey toward the sea: one flows through the southern China, the other through the northern China.

Adapted and Revised from The Rushing Yellow River **by Luo Shuyun and Zhao Heshun**

The Swan Lake

China's Swan Lake (also known as the Bayanbulak Lake) is located in the Bayanbulak Plan in Xinjiang and is a mountain lake, surrounded by ice mountains of the Tianshan. The Swan Lake is 30 kilometers long from east to west and 10 kilometers wide from south to north, with many clear springs around it. In spring, snow melts and flows in the lake, which has clear water and spectacular views. Each spring, a large amount of swans will fly from India and the southern part of Africa where they spend the entire winter to the lake for breeding. During this season, there are hundreds of thousands of swans on the lake: some are swimming freely on the lake, some are building nest and hatching eggs in the grass at the lakeside. The tundra swans can run, swim and find food in the lake like their parents three or four hours after coming out of the shell. They grow fast and will weigh about 10 kilograms in three months.

The Swan Lake is one of the areas with the most swans in the world. In 1986, in order to protect the swans here, Chinese government treated the place as the Swan Nature Reserve.

第二课

黄河的源头（二）

黄河从它的北部发源地的涓涓细流汇成一条河流后，越过约古宗列盆地，首先流进了星宿海。

星宿海并不是什么波涛滚滚的大海，它只是一个长20千米～30千米，宽约10多千米，四周都是山地的积水盆地。盆地里散布着数不清的大大小小的"海子"（湖泊），大的面积有几百平方米，小的只有几平方米。站在附近的山头上远远看去，这些"海子"在阳光的照射下，好像无数面大小不一的镜子，闪闪发光，就像天上的星星都跑到这里来歇宿(sù)似的。"星宿海"这个美丽的名字就是这样得来的。

黄河在星宿海里散(sǎn)乱地流过，一会儿分成几支，一会儿又合成一条，在那些大大小小的湖泊中穿来穿去，没有正式的河道，这就是过去认为黄河发源于星宿海的原因。穿过星宿海之后，黄河向东流进了扎陵湖和鄂陵湖①。

扎陵湖和鄂陵湖是青海南部高原上两个著名的淡水湖，也

---

① 扎陵湖——藏语，意思是"灰白色的长湖"。
鄂陵湖——藏语，意思是"青蓝色的长湖"。

是整个黄河流域内两个最大的湖泊。它们的海拔高度达4000多米。扎陵湖的水浅，平均水深只有八九米。由于黄河和其他河流带来了很多的泥沙，湖水变成灰白色。

鄂陵湖比扎陵湖大，水也比较深，水深差不多是扎陵湖的两倍（平均水深17.6米），河流带进来的泥沙不容易把水弄浑，因此，湖水的颜色总是蓝蓝的。在一般的地图上，这两个湖泊小得很，可是，如果你到湖边看看的话，一眼望不到边的湖水，随风而起的阵阵波涛，你一定会以为到了无边无际的大海了。每当风和日丽，湖水平静的时候，四周白色的雪山，天空飘浮的白云，全都倒映在蓝色的湖面上，就像一幅美丽的图画。

再来说说水鸟吧！鄂陵湖中有三个小岛，岛上住着20多种水鸟，其中最多的是天鹅、仙鹤和大雁等。它们

鄂陵湖

都把自己的窝建在岛上的岩石缝中，远远望去，就像一层层的楼房似的。它们当中有候鸟，也有留鸟。每年5月前后，天气转暖，头一年冬天飞到南方去过冬的候鸟们，总是按时回到这里。它们和那些留鸟们共同把小岛变成了一个热闹、拥挤的鸟的世界。如果6月前后你乘船来到这些小岛上，就会看到地上到处是

成堆的鸟蛋。但是，想拿这些鸟蛋可要小心，如果被水鸟发现了，它们会叫着向你冲来，有时还会不停地在你头上拉下鸟粪，直到你把鸟蛋放下以后才散去。在这些水鸟中，有许多是非常珍贵的种类，例如黑颈鹤等。生活在岛上的水鸟，大都是捕鱼的能手。平常它们总是在清澈(chè)的湖面上不停地飞来飞去，有时飞着飞着，突然冲下水去，一口就叼住一条活鱼。

除了这些水鸟以外，湖里的鱼也不少。这些鱼和我们平常见到的鱼不大一样，都是无鳞鱼。它们长期生活在气候寒冷的高原湖水中，一点也不怕冷，可是生长都很缓慢，七八年才能长到一斤重。高原湖区人烟稀少，因此鱼儿们一点也不知道害怕人，整天在湖水中自由地游来游去，当你走近湖边时，它们还会成群结队地向你游来。在这里捕鱼可太容易了，一网就可以拉上五六百斤。就是钓鱼，十分钟也可以钓到七八条之多。

黄河像一条灰白色的带子从湖心穿过，把蓝蓝的湖水分为两半，然后从鄂陵湖北端出湖，向东南流去，经过四川、甘肃又流回青海的龙羊峡①。从这里开始，黄河走完了它的河源段，进入了上游峡谷区。

（根据罗枢运、赵合顺《奔腾的黄河》改编）

---

① 龙羊峡——地名。

生词

juān juān 涓涓	trickling (stream)	dà yàn 大雁	wild goose
huì hé 汇（合）	converge	yōng jǐ 拥挤	congested; packed
è líng hú 鄂陵湖	Eling Lake	fèn 粪	excrement; droppings
liǎng bèi 两倍	twice	lín piàn 鳞（片）	scale (of fish, etc.)
hún 浑	muddy	diào yú 钓鱼	fish; angle
dào yìng 倒映	mirror; reflect		

听写

汇成　波涛　两倍　倒映　大雁　拥挤　鸟粪　钓鱼　鳞　＊鄂陵湖

比一比

浑（浑水）
挥（挥手）
辉（光辉）

除 { 除了 / 除害 / 大扫除 }

散 { 散乱 / 零散 }

字词运用

把……弄浑　挥手　光辉

请不要把水弄浑!

火车开动了,爸爸在窗口向我挥手告别。

这一小片乌云遮不住太阳的光辉。

除了……以外　除害　大扫除

我们家除了弟弟以外,都戴眼镜。

李寄杀蛇,为民除了害。

春节前许多人家做大扫除,迎接新春。

整齐　拥挤

作业要写得干净、整齐。

上海的南京路十分拥挤。

倍

这块地的面积是那块地的三倍。

我们的书比你们的多一倍。

多音字

缝 fèng
石头缝 fèng

缝 féng
缝衣服 féng

宿 xiù
星宿 xiù

宿 sù
住宿 sù

词语解释

歇宿——休息过夜。

风和日丽——微风轻轻地吹，太阳很明亮，形容天气很好。

人烟稀少——住户很少。

成群结队——一群一群的，一队一队的，形容数量很多。

盐 湖

很久以前,青藏高原是一片海洋,经过亿万年的地壳运动,青藏高原上升,原来低洼(wā)处留下的海水就形成了盐湖。中国青海省柴达木盆地的察尔汗盐池,是中国最大的盐湖。湖上结了一层厚厚的盐盖,就像水晶镜面一样。这里的公路、铁路都直接建在盐湖上。通往西藏的青藏公路和青藏铁路,便是在盐盖上通过的,被人们称为"万丈盐桥"。

柴达木盆地的盐湖

Lesson Two

The Source of the Yellow River (II)

The Yellow River gathers several streamlets to north of its source, flows through the Yueguzonglie Basin and then into the Star Sea.

The Star Sea is no surfy ocean; it is merely a ponding basin surrounded by mountain areas. It is 20 to 30 kilometers long and about 10 kilometers wide, with numerous lakes scattered in it. The area of the big lakes is several hundred square meters, while that of the small ones is only several square meters. Standing at the top of a surrounding mountain and looking down, you will see numerous mirrors of different sizes below, flashing and shining under the sunlight like stars and hence its beautiful name of the Star Sea.

The Yellow River flows through the Star Sea randomly, dividing here into several branches and joining together there. It meanders through the Star Sea without a fixed river course, which partly contributes to the former assumption that the Yellow River originates from the Star Sea. Leaving the Star Sea behind, the Yellow River then flows eastward into the Gyaring Lake and the Eling Lake.

The Gyaring Lake and the Eling Lake are two famous fresh lakes on the Qinghai Plateau and the largest lakes within the entire Yellow River basin. They are 4,000 meters high above the sea level. The water depth of the Gyaring Lake is shallow and the average depth is eight to nine meters. Since the Yellow River and other rivers bring a lot of sand and mud, the color of the lake is ash grey.

The Eling Lake is larger than the Gyaring Lake and the water is deeper (the average water depth is 17.6 meters) and almost twice deeper than the Gyaring Lake. Accordingly, it is not easy for the sand and mud brought along by the rivers to make the water muddy and the lake is always blue. These two lakes might appear small on the ordinary map; but if you stand at the lakeside, you will think that you are at the seaside; for the other shore is out of your sight and great waves surge with the wind. When the weather is fine and the sun shines brightly, the calm blue lake mirrors surrounding white snow mountains as well as the white fluffy clouds in the sky, producing a breathtakingly beautiful picture.

Let's now turn our eyes on the water birds here. In the Eling Lake there are three islets inhabited by more than 20 types of water birds, among which swans, cranes and wild geese are the most. They build their nests in rock cracks on the islet, resembling buildings arranged in stories. Some of these birds are migratory birds and some are resident birds. Around May each year when it becomes warmer, the migratory birds flying to the south in the previous winter will return to this area on time and create, together with all resident birds, a bustling and rustling world of birds. If you visit the islets by boat around June, you will see piles of bird eggs here. You'd better be careful when you pick up these eggs; for if you are found by the birds, they will charge at you, screaming at you and even attacking you with droppings, till you put down their eggs. Among these water fowls, some are rare species, such as black-necked

cranes.Most of the water birds living on the islets are expert fishers. They always fly above the clear water, dive into the water and seldom miss the target.

Apart from the water fowls, there are a lot of fishes in the lake. The fishes here are not the same with those we see in ordinary everyday life; for they are high land cold water scaleless fishes that live in cold highland lake. They are accustomed to the cold weather yet grow slowly at the speed of gaining 500 grams every seven to eight years. There are a few people frequent the highland lake area, accordingly, the fishes here will not be scared away at the sight of human beings. They swim freely in the lake and will even swarm toward you if you come close to the lake. It is an easy task to catch fish here and a single casting of the net can get 250 to 300 kilograms fishes. An ordinary angler can easily get seven to eight fishes within ten minutes.

The Yellow River flows through the center of the lake like an ash grey ribbon, dividing the blue lake water into two halves. Then it leaves the Eling Lake at its north outlet and flows to the southeast through Sichuan and Gansu Province before returning to the Longyang Gorge of Qinghai Province. This is the end of the source section of the Yellow River. From here on, it enters its upper reach in canyon area.

Adapted and Revised from *The Rushing Yellow River* by Luo Shuyun and Zhao Heshun

The Salt Lake

Long time ago, the Qinghai-Xizang Plateau used to be an ocean. After hundreds of millions years of earth movement, the plateau rises while the sea water left in the low ground forms salt lakes. The Qarhan Salt Lake in Caidam Basin of Qinghai Province is the largest salt lake in China. There is a thick layer of salt crust covered the lake surface; the crust is shiny like crystal mirror. All the roads and railways here are constructed directly on the salt lake; the Qinghai-Xizang Road and Qinghai-Xizang Railway passes through the salt crust, which is known as the "lofty salt bridge."

第三课

银杏和水杉

（一）古老的树种——银杏

银杏树是中国特有的珍贵树种，它长得又高又大，满树绿绿的叶子，像一把把小折扇，迎风抖动。

银杏树是非常古老的树种，早在两亿七千万年以前，银杏树就出现在地球上了。它们与恐龙一块儿生活过。一亿多年以前，银杏的家族大得很，地球上到处都有银杏树，而且有好几种。后来，地球上发生了冰川运动，银杏在欧洲、北美全部灭绝，埋在了地底下，成了化石，只有一小部分在中国留存至今。因此，科学家们叫它"活化石"。

银杏树枝与恐龙化石

银杏的衰亡，像其他许多古代植物一样，是地球历史变化的结果，另外，也有它本身的原因。银杏有个俗名叫"公孙树"，意思就是说，爷爷种下树苗，到了孙子才能吃到果子，说明它是一种生长很慢的树木。再有一个原因，银杏是雌雄异株的。雄的银杏树，只长雄性的花；雌的银杏树，只长雌性的花。如果一个地方只有雄树，或者只有雌树，这里的银杏树就无法结果，也就不能很好地繁殖了。

银杏，也叫白果，是落叶乔木，一般可做绿化树，它的果仁可以食用，也可以入药，但吃多了会中毒。

银杏的木材结实又不怕虫子蛀，是优良的建筑材料，又可以用来制作家具，可惜产量太少了。而银杏最大的价值还是在科学上，通过它可以研究生物进化、地质演化、古代气候……总之，在很多科学研究中，银杏都是难得的材料。

（二）珍贵植物——水杉

在中国各地的植物园、公园或学校，有时会见到一种秀丽而古雅的树木，它的名字叫水杉。

植物学家与古生物学家的研究证明，水杉为古老的植物之一。全世界只有中国还有水杉，在别的国家，水杉早已经绝种了，所以人们称它为"稀有的植物"或者"活化石"。

远在一亿多年以前，水杉的祖先就诞生于北极圈了。当时地球上气候非常温暖，北极也不像现在那样全都是冰雪。后来，由于气候的变化，地质的变迁，水杉逐渐分布到了欧、亚和北美三大洲，特别是在中欧，几乎到处都是。到了第四纪，由于地球上生成了大片的冰川，水杉等植物经受不住寒冷，在欧洲、北美全部灭绝了。

水杉

当时冰川在中国分布也很广。科学家们发现，中国华东、华中、华南到处可以找到冰川的遗迹。不过中国的第四纪冰川，与欧美的冰川不一样，不是成片的，而是东一块西一块，各块不相连的"山地冰川"，因此，中国有许多地区未受冰川的严重影响，一小部分水杉得以保存了下来。四川、湖北交界一带就成了它们的"避难所"。从此，它们就一直默默无闻地生长在中国的深山里，而在欧美，人们只能从地层中挖掘到它的化石。

1941年，中国有一位教授在四川万县磨刀溪发现了三株稀有松柏类植物。后来又在湖北利川县发现几百株同样的植物。它们叫什么？属于哪一科？哪一属？当时谁也不知道。直到1945年，才由中国的植物分类学家和树木学家共同研究确定了它们是松柏类中的孑遗植物——水杉。

生词

dǒu dòng 抖动	shake	jìn huà 进化	evolve
kǒng lóng 恐龙	dinosaur	dì zhì 地质	geology
shuāi wáng 衰亡	decline	yǎn huà 演化	evolve
cí xióng yì zhū 雌雄异株	dioecious	gǔ yǎ 古雅	of classic elegance
fán zhí 繁殖	reproduce	bì nàn suǒ 避难所	shelter
qiáo mù 乔木	arbor	wā jué 挖掘	excavate
guǒ rén 果仁	kernel	xī 溪	brook
kě xī 可惜	regrettable; unfortunately	jié yí zhí wù 孑遗植物	surviving plant

听写

抖动　雌雄异株　果仁　乔木　挖掘　溪　可惜

恐龙　繁殖　*演化

比一比

折 { 折断 / 折扇 }　　苗 { 树苗 / 麦苗 }　　{ 殖（繁殖）/ 值（价值）}

化 { 演化 / 进化 }　　质 { 地质 / 石灰质 }　　子 { 子（孑遗）/ 子（儿子）}

字词运用

诞生　延长

一亿多年前，水杉的祖先就诞生于北极圈了。

现在人们的生活水平提高了，寿命也延长了。

乔木　大桥　骄傲　娇气

银杏是落叶乔木。

如果你去旧金山，一定要看看金门大桥。

虚心使人进步，骄傲使人落后。

小妹妹一点也不娇气，摔倒了，自己爬起来。

打斗　抖动　蝌蚪

学校里不允许打斗。

微风吹来，树叶轻轻抖动。

蝌蚪要找妈妈，但是不知道妈妈长什么样。

繁殖

有一些海鱼是游到河里繁殖后代的。

银杏树雌雄异株,所以繁殖比较困难。

近义词

逐渐——渐渐　　　灭绝——消失

反义词

优良——差　　　异——同

词语解释

灭绝——完全消灭,不存在了。

俗名——通俗的名称,不是正式的名称。

优良——(品种、质量、成绩、作风等)很好。

逐渐——渐渐。

遗迹——古代事物留下来的痕迹。

默默无闻——不出名,没人知道。

阅读

长在虫子身上的"草"

你见过"冬虫夏草"吗？这种草很稀奇，上边是根草，下边是条虫子。这草怎么长到虫子身上去了呢？为什么偏偏长在一种虫子身上？

冬虫夏草生长在北温带海拔三四千米的高原上，它们一般生长在灌木丛(cóng)里或草甸(diàn)子上。只有在春天，冻(dòng)土刚刚融化的时候，才能在山上找到冬虫夏草。这种草和那些绿色的、会开花结果的草不一样，它是一种菌类，像蘑菇(mó gu)一样，自己不能制造养料，不能独立生活。所以，它找到蝙蝠蛾(é)的幼(yòu)虫，就寄生在这种虫子身上，吸收虫子体内的养料，自己长大了，可是虫子却被它吸干了。冬天的时候，还是一条虫子，而夏天来到时，虫子身上却长出了像草似的菌丝，虫子和草连在一块儿，不能分开，因此才得了"冬虫夏草"这么个奇怪的名字。

冬虫夏草是很难得的药材，能治许多病。

冬虫夏草

Lesson Three

The Maidenhair Tree and the Metasequoia

I. An Ancient Species: the Maidenhair Tree

The maidenhair tree is a unique and precious species in China. Its trunk is tall, its crown spreads extensively, and its thick green leaves are like small folding fans, waving in the wind.

The maidenhair tree is an ancient species and appeared on the earth 270 million years ago. They used to be under the same sky with dinosaurs. More than one hundred million years ago, the family of maidenhair trees was large and had several different species, covering the entire world. Later on, the glacier movement occurred; they became extinct in both Europe and North America, were buried underground and turned into fossils. Only a small part of the family survived in China and lived till this day. Therefore, scientists call it "living fossil."

The declining of the maidenhair tree is, just as many other ancient plants, the result of the changes of the earth. In addition, it has its own inherent reasons. One is the maidenhair tree is also known as the gong-sun tree (the grandpa-grandson tree) in China, which means that the tree grows so slow that after a grandpa plants a tree only his grandson can eat its fruits. The other reason is that the maidenhair tree is dioecious: a tree yields either staminate flowers or pistillate flowers. Therefore, if there are only male trees or female trees in a place, then there will be no fruits and accordingly no reproduction.

The maidenhair tree is deciduous and can serve as afforestation species. Its fruits are edible gingko nuts; it can be used as a medicine, though a large amount of intaking will cause poisoning.

The wood of maidenhair trees is solid and moth-free, serves as the best construction material and can be used to make furniture; it's a pity that its production is limited. But its value mostly lies in scientific research, for it is a precious material in the study of biological evolution, geological changes and ancient climate, etc.

II. A Precious Plant: the Metasequoia

When you visit botanical gardens, parks or schools in China, you will see a beautiful and elegant tree species; its name is metasequoia.

According to the research made by botanists and paleontologists, the metasequoia is one of the most ancient plants on earth and has become extinct in the world except in China. Therefore, people often call it "rare plant" or "living fossil."

As early as more than 100 million years ago, the ancient metasequoia has been appeared within the Arctic Circle. At that time, the climate on earth was very warm and the North Pole was not covered by ice and snow as it is now. Later on, along with the changes of the climate and geology, the metasequoia has been spread into three main continents of Europe, Asia and North America. It could be found almost all over the Central Europe. During the Quaternary Period, since there was a large amount of glacier on earth, many plants including the metasequoia could not stand the coldness and became extinct in both Europe and North America.

At that time, the distribution of glaciers used to be extensive in China and scientists found traces of glaciers in eastern, middle and southern China. It is noticeable that the glaciers in China of the Quaternary Period were not the same as those in Europe and America, where the glacier is one huge block. In China, they were upland glaciers scattered here and there without being joined together. Accordingly, many areas have not been severely affected in China and a small part of the metasequoia survived. Some found shelters in the boundary areas of Sichuan and Hubei Province and have lived in the valleys there since then, unknown to the public; while in Europe and America, only its fossil can be discovered deep under the ground.

In 1941, a Chinese professor found three rare coniferous trees along the Modao Brook of Wanxian County in Sichuan Province. Later on, several hundred plants of the same species have been found in Lichuan County of Hubei Province. What is the name of these plants and which section or species do they belong to? No one knew at that time. It was not until 1945 when, after joint research, Chinese plant Methodists and dendrologists decided that they were metasequoia, the surviving plant of coniferles.

The "Grass" Growing out of Worms

Have you ever seen Dong-chong-xia-cao (Chinese Caterpillar Fungus)? The grass-like fungus looks strange, for its upper part is a leaf of grass, yet its lower part is a caterpillar. Then how comes and why does the fungus grow out of caterpillar?

The Chinese caterpillar fungus grows among the shrub and on the grassy marshland of three to four thousand meters above sea level within the North Temperate Zone. It can only be found during spring time in the mountains immediately after the frozen soil melts. It is not the same with those green grass that flowers and yields fruits; it is actually a kind of fungus, like mushrooms, which cannot produce nourishment and live independently. So it has to find larva of ghost moths and parasitizes on it. The fungus lives on the larva and absorbs its nourishment; after the fungus grows up, the larva has been sucked dry. Therefore, a caterpillar in the winter produces grass-like fungus in the summer and both of them connect closely together; hence the strange name of "caterpillar in winter and grass in summer".

The fungus is a rare medicinal material and is effective in curing many kinds of diseases.

第四课

跳 伞

一架飞机飞到机场上空，突然，从飞机里跳出了5个小黑点。只见那小黑点越掉越快。5秒钟后，5顶降落伞几乎同时张开，不一会儿，运动员平安地降落在机场上。这是"迟缓跳伞"表演。

一会儿飞机又飞回来了。这次飞机里跳出10个小黑点，10顶降落伞马上张开了，像10朵小蘑菇，在天空飘浮。10多分钟以后，她们降落在机场上。

最后是集群跳伞，有100位运动员参加。

飞机里跳出一连串的黑点来，降落伞跟着张开了。这次每个运动员带着两顶伞。大的一顶是白色的，小的一顶颜色各不相同：有红的、黄的…… 一时间，蓝蓝的天空中好像开满了五颜六色的花朵。

紧张的两分钟

跳伞运动员必须有健壮的体格，熟练的技巧，更重要的是必须有坚强的意志。就拿"迟缓跳伞"来说吧，有的跳伞运动员能下落到离地面200米的时候才打开降落伞。要是飞机在2000米的高空飞行，运动员跳出机舱降落到地面，前后用不了两分钟

的时间。我们很难想象在这两分钟里，他有多紧张。一跳出飞机，他下落的速度就越来越快。根据物理公式来算，在第一秒钟末，速度接近每秒10米；在第二秒钟末，速度接近每秒20米。照这样，只需半分钟，他下落的速度就比音速还快了。还好，实际上并非如此。物理公式指的是物体在真空中下落的情形，而跳伞是在空气中进行的，我们得把空气的阻力计算在内。

在空气中，物体往下掉得越快，来自空气的阻力就越大。当继续增加的速度正好跟空气的阻力相抵消时，物体就不会越掉越快了。以跳伞运动员来说，大概他跳出飞机十一二秒钟之后，下落的速度就不再增加，保持在每秒50米～60米之间。就算每秒50米，1分钟就得下落3000米，比火车的速度快两三倍。因此，跳伞运动员必须头脑清醒，要不然就会摔死。

快！打开降落伞

他没有依靠，一直往下掉。时间过得飞快，地面迅速地向他迎上来，500米，400米……250米，准备，200米，快！动作要敏捷！打开降落伞，不能晚1秒钟。这1秒之差（chā），就决定了他能

不能安全落地。降落伞从打开到张满大约要用两秒钟。在这两秒钟里，他还得往下掉100米。等到降落伞完全张开的时候，他离地面只有100米了。要是晚打开1秒钟，降落伞就会来不及张满，后果将是十分可怕的。不过，降落伞一旦张满，下降的速度马上就减小了，从每秒钟五六十米，一下子减到每秒钟五六米。我们乘火车和汽车，都有这样的经验：火车、汽车开得很快的时候，要是猛一刹车，身体就会向前面冲去。降落伞张满的时候，跳伞运动员也有这样的感觉，可是力量要比刹车时大四五倍。这个震动一下就过去了，不会使他强健的身体受伤。挂在张满的降落伞下面就安全多了。可是他还得注意风向和风力的大小，注意地面上的情况，控制降落伞带，使自己不要落在河里，不要落在树上。快到地面时，他必须做好准备：两条腿并好，屈起膝盖，这样腿在落地时，才不会受伤。

必须这样做

如果一跳出飞机就打开降落伞，当然安全多了。可是在打仗时，伞兵常常采用"迟缓跳伞"，尽量落到离地面200米时再打开伞。因为战争中，运送伞兵的飞机必须飞得很高，离地五六千米，才能躲开敌人炮火的射击。要是伞兵一跳出飞机就打开伞，他们在空中要飘几十分钟才能落到地面。风可能把他们吹

到很远的地方，也可能把队伍吹散。再说降落伞要是慢慢地往下落，就容易被敌人用枪打中。为了安全，伞兵必须要掌握"迟缓跳伞"的技术。

生词

yùn dòng yuán 运动员	sportsman	miǎo 秒	second
jiàng luò 降落	descend; land	zǔ lì 阻力	resistance
chí huǎn 迟缓	tardy; delay	dà gài 大概	approximately
biǎo yǎn 表演	performance	xùn sù 迅速	rapid
mó gu 蘑菇	mushroom	shā chē 刹车	brake
jǐn zhāng 紧张	nervous; intense	kòng zhì 控制	control
shú liàn 熟练	proficient	xī gài 膝盖	knee
jì qiǎo 技巧	technique	pào 炮	artillery
gōng shì 公式	equation	zhǎng wò 掌握	master

听写

降落　炮　表演　技巧　公式　熟练　紧张　掌握　大概

迅速　秒　*刹车　控制

比一比

炮 { 大炮 / 炮兵 / 炮弹 }　　迟 { 迟到 / 迟缓 / 迟早 }　　式 { 形式 / 公式 / 各式各样 }　　紧 { 紧张 / 紧急 / 松紧 }

速 { 迅速 / 速度 }　　掌 { 掌握 / 手掌 }　　依 { 依靠 / 依然 }　　阻 { 阻力 / 阻挡 }

字词运用

依靠

要学会独立生活，不能事事依靠父母。

陈英是个盲人，但她依靠自己的努力，成为一名调(tiáo)琴师。

掌握

王浩(hào)勤学好问，很快他就掌握了种菜的技术。

尽量

奶奶年龄太大了,听力不好,请你说话尽量慢一点、清楚一点。

大概

这次篮球比赛我们学校大概能赢。

从上海到旧金山的往返机票大概八百美元。

反义词

降落——起飞　　　安全——危险　　　迟缓——敏捷

多音字

尽 jǐn　　　　　　　尽 jìn

尽 jǐn { 尽量 jǐn / 尽管 jǐn }　　　尽 jìn { 尽力 jìn / 尽头 jìn }

差 chā　　　　　　　差 chà

一秒之差 chā　　　　差不多 chà

词语解释

技巧——表现在艺术、工艺、体育等方面的巧妙的技能。

并非如此——并不是这样。

抵消——两种事物的作用因相反而互相消除。

阅读

时间伯伯

时间伯伯，
你是一个飞行员，
不停地在飞行。
你飞过宇宙的每一个角落，
从白天飞到黑夜，
又从黑夜飞向天明。

时间伯伯，
我们不知道你有多少岁数，
你好像没有开始也没有尽头。
你是一位老者，同时也是一位少年，
你比最古老的岩石还要古老，
你比最年轻的生命还要年轻。

时间伯伯,

钟表滴答滴答的声音,

是你的脚步声。

中国古人说:"时间如流水,一去不复返。"

又说:"一寸光阴一寸金。"

你的每一分、每一秒,

都是这样宝贵,

我们一定爱惜你,

像爱惜自己的生命。

(根据高士其《时间伯伯》改编)

回答问题

请说一说:你对"一寸光阴一寸金"这句话怎么看?

Lesson Four

Parachute Jump

An airplane flew above the airfield and suddenly, five small black objects dropped out of the plane and fell directly downward to the ground. After five seconds, five parachutes opened almost at the same time and the five parachuters landed on the field safely in a while. This was a performance of "accelerated freefall parachute jump."

After a while, the plane flew back and this time ten parachuters jumped out of the plane with ten parachutes opening immediately. Ten small mushrooms floated in the sky for more than ten minutes before finally touching the ground.

The last performance was group jumping with one hundred participants.

A string of black dots came out of the plane and the parachutes opened immediately after the parachuters dived into the sky. This time, each parachuter had two parachutes: the big ones were white while the small ones were in various kinds of colors including red and yellow.... For a while, it seemed that many colorful flowers dotted the blue sky.

The Most Intense Two Minutes

A parachuter must have healthy body, proficient skill, and most importantly strong will. Taking accelerated freefall parachute jump as example, some parachuters dive into the sky for a free fall and only open their parachutes 200 meters above the field. If the plane flies at a 2,000-meter level, it takes no more than two minutes for the parachuters to touch the ground. It is hard for us to imagine how intense a freefall parachuter might experience during the two minutes. At jumping out of the plane, the speed he falls is faster and faster. Calculated according to applicable physical equation, at the end of the first second, the falling velocity is close to 10 meters per second; at the end of the second second, the falling velocity is close to 20 meters per second. In this manner, it takes only half minutes for an accelerated freefall parachuter to exceed sonic speed. Fortunately, this is not the case in reality, for this physical equation applies to the freefall in vacuum. Since the actual parachute jump is conducted in the air, we have to calculate the air resistance.

In the air, the faster an object falls, the bigger the air resistance; when the increase of speed offsets the air resistance, then the falling speed will remain the same. As for a parachuter, eleven or twelve seconds after he jumps out of the plane, the falling velocity will not increase any more and keeps at 50-60 meters per second. But even it is 50 meters per second, it means a fall of 3,000 meters in one minute and two or three times more than the speed of a train. Therefore, the parachuter must stay calm and be sober; otherwise, he will die hitting the ground.

Open Your Parachute, Now !

He is a freely falling body now and falls down from the sky. Time flies and the ground becomes nearer and nearer. 500 meters, 400 meters... 250 meters, get ready, 200 meters, now! open your parachute and even one second delay is not allowed, for this is the second that decides whether he can land safely on the ground. It takes about two seconds for a parachute to completely open. During this two seconds, he will fall another one hundred meters, which means that he is only 100 meters above the ground when the parachute opens and works. If there is one second delay and the parachute can not fully open, the mistake might be fatal. Once the parachute opens, the falling speed reduces immediately from 50-60 meters per second to 5-6 meters per second. We all have this experience by taking train and car: if a driver brakes a fast going train or car, people inside will dash forward. It is the same with the parachuter when the parachute opens, only that the force is four or five times more than that you experience from your daily ride. The jolt comes and goes quickly and does not do any harm to his healthy body. Although now it is much safer hanging below the fully opened parachute, yet he must still pay attention to the direction and power of the wind, to the ground conditions. He must steer the control string of the para-

chute to land himself on appropriate location, not into the river or on the tree. When a parachuter is about to land, he has to prepare for the landing by putting together and folding his legs to avoid possible injury.

You Have to Do It

It is of course safer to open the parachute at jumping out of the plane. But during wartime, the paratroopers usually choose accelerated freefall parachute jump and wait till 200 meters above the ground to open their parachutes, for the planes carrying paratroopers have to fly high at five or six thousand meters to avoid the antiaircraft artillery of the enemy. If the paratroopers open their parachutes once out of the plane, it will take them dozens of minutes to land on the ground. For one thing, the wind might carry them far away from the destination and the troop might scatter in a large area. For another, the parachutes are big targets and the soldiers hanging below it are easily to be shot by enemies. Therefore, for the sake of safeness, the paratroopers have to master the skill of accelerated freefall parachute jump.

Uncle Time

Uncle Time,
You are a pilot,
Flying unceasingly.
You fly through every corner of the universe,
Flying from day to night,
Then from night to day once again.

Uncle Time,
We don't know how old you are,
It seems that you have no starting point and no ending.
You are both an old man and a youngster,
You are older than the oldest rock,
You are younger than the youngest life.

Uncle Time,
The ticktack of the clock,
Is your footstep.
Ancient Chinese say: "Time is the running water and never comes back."
They also say: "Time is measured by gold."
Every minute and every second
Is so precious;
We will treasure you
As we treasure our lives.

Adapted and Revised from *Uncle Time* by Gao Shiqi

第五课

野骆驼

人们都知道大熊猫,但很少有人听说过野骆驼。其实,世界上野骆驼的数量仅剩下800只左右,比大熊猫还少,它们和大熊猫一样,都是非常珍稀的动物。

野骆驼是原生种

早在中国的汉代,就有了关于骆驼的记载。明朝李时珍在《本草纲目》中也分别提到野驼与家驼。

野骆驼

现在世界上有六种骆驼:原驼、骆马、美洲驼、羊驼、单峰驼和双峰驼。原驼、骆马现在还是野生状态,美洲驼、羊驼和单峰驼都是饲养种了。而双峰驼呢,大部分为家畜,只有一小部分还处于野生状态。它们分布在中国新疆、甘肃和蒙古国境内。

以前，动物学界认为双峰驼都已驯化为家畜，世界上已经没有野生种了。19世纪末叶，在中国新疆罗布泊以东，阿尔金山以北地区发现了野生双峰骆驼，这引起动物学界的重视。1980年，中国科学院派人考察了罗布泊，见到了许多野骆驼。研究证明，在中国生存的野生双峰驼为原生的野生种，并不是家驼的野化种。

荒漠上的流浪汉

中国的珍稀野生动物中，野骆驼的生存环境在全世界大概也是最为恶劣的。它们仅有的栖息地都在亚洲中部最干旱的沙漠地区，最低气温是摄氏零下49度，最高气温为摄氏55度，地表温度最高在摄氏70度以上。这里没有淡水，有的只是又苦又咸的盐泉；大部分地区寸草不生，只在盐泉附近长着稀稀拉拉的盐生草。野骆驼生活在这样的环境中，吃的是几乎没有叶子的植物，喝的是盐水，以日月为友，与风沙为伴。

野骆驼并不是喜欢喝盐水，而是因为受到人类的逼迫，逃进了荒凉的戈壁滩。在那里，有盐水从地下咕嘟咕嘟冒上来。野骆

驼就喝这种盐水，它的肝竟然也慢慢适应了这种情况。世界上没有其他动物能有这种本领，其实就连野骆驼自己也不容易，好些两岁以下的小骆驼就因为肝不能适应而死去。为了适应生存环境，野骆驼在生理上也发生了很大的变化。在不喝一滴水的情况下，野骆驼能在炎热的沙漠里行走两个星期。这时它的体重会下降到原来的3/4。有水的时候，它们又可以在几分钟之内喝下多达200千克的水。动物学家说，对一般动物来说，这种体内水分(fèn)的剧烈变化，对生命是很危险的，但野骆驼能让身体快速补充水分，因而能在沙漠里生存。

人们观察野骆驼时会发现：一只雄性野骆驼往往带着一群骆驼，包括十多只雌骆驼和它们的小骆驼。为了争夺雌骆驼，雄骆驼们会打架，打败的那只有时会走上150千米去找别的雌骆驼。在交配期后，雄骆驼会离开驼群。在每年的三四月，你会看到一些孤单的雄性野骆驼四处游荡，但它们不会离开家人太远，一旦发现危险，就会跑回去保护雌骆驼和小骆驼。过13个月以后，雌骆驼也会悄悄地离开驼群去生小骆驼。

野骆驼还有个有趣之处，就是能够几百年来沿着同一条道路

迁徙。野骆驼的脚印从一个盐水泉伸向另一个盐水泉。当盐水泉边的植物吃完时，它们就迁向别处。这些野骆驼总是排成一队沿着老路走。你会看到有一条非常明显的、骆驼踩出的小路，一直伸向阿尔金山。野骆驼每年都要经过这条路，到阿尔金山的阴凉山谷里，躲避夏季沙漠的高温；冬天，它们又走回到沙漠的中心地带。

春天天气虽然暖和，可是另一个威胁又来了，那就是说来就来的沙漠风暴，当地人称为黄沙暴和黑沙暴。黄沙暴刮起时，漫天的黄沙能遮挡住太阳，使周围的东西看上去都是金黄色的；而黑沙暴更可怕，当它来临时，白天就变成了黑夜，沙子、石头随风乱飞。这时，可怜的骆驼只能伸着长脖子躺在地上。

野骆驼

野骆驼还有个本领就是会哭。其实，骆驼都会流眼泪，泪水从它长长的睫(jié)毛下流出来。骆驼在沙暴中肯定很不舒服，但它不是因为难过而哭，而是它正在用泪水将眼里的沙子冲洗出来。它还有长长的鼻翼保护着鼻腔，所以在沙尘暴中也能够呼吸。

救救野骆驼

作为一个古老的物种,野骆驼能在如此严酷的环境中生存下来,这本身就是奇迹。大自然给了我们这么宝贵的物种,而我们对它的关心又有多少呢?

如今对野骆驼最大的威胁是人。过去,当地居民一直有捕食野骆驼的习惯。现在有了野生动物保护法,禁止猎杀野骆驼,可是放牧的范围不断扩张,野骆驼的栖息地越来越小,寻找食物越来越困难。山中的野狼也威胁着野骆驼的安全。天灾人祸使野骆驼越来越少。一百年前还有一万多只,到了1980年的时候,野骆驼减少到2000~3000只,目前仅有800只左右了。

到目前为止,有关野骆驼的电视片、照片都少得可怜。1993年,中国发行了第一套野骆驼的邮票。希望将来我们的子孙后代,不要只能从邮票上才看得到野骆驼。

生字

luò tuo 骆驼	camel	jiāo pèi 交配	mate
sì yǎng 饲养	raise	qiān xǐ 迁徙	migrate
jiā chù 家畜	livestock	wēi xié 威胁	threat
zhuàng tài 状态	status	fēng bào 风暴	storm
xùn huà 驯化	domesticate	shū fu 舒服	comfortable
huán jìng 环境	enviroment	bí yì 鼻翼	nose wing
è liè 恶劣	harsh; vile	bí qiāng 鼻腔	nasal cavity
qī xī dì 栖息地	habitat	yán kù 严酷	harsh
shè shì 摄氏	centigrade	jìn zhǐ 禁止	forbid
shì yìng 适应	adjust, adapt	fàn wéi 范围	scope
bǔ chōng 补充	replenish	tiān zāi rén huò 天灾人祸	natural and man-made calamities

听写

骆驼　环境　家畜　威胁　禁止　恶劣　补充　舒服

范围　风暴　*摄氏　天灾人祸

比一比

适 { 适应 / 适合 }　　摄 { 摄氏 / 摄影 }　　{ 暴（风暴）/ 爆（爆炸）}

态 { 状态 / 态度 }　　围 { 范围 / 周围 }　　{ 饲（饲养）/ 司（司机）}

补 { 补充 / 补习 }　　票 { 邮票 / 车票 }　　{ 境（环境）/ 竟（竟然）}

字词运用

威胁

核武器威胁着世界和平。

肥胖正威胁着人们的健康。

本领

野骆驼有让身体快速补充水分的本领。

伞兵必须要掌握"迟缓跳伞"的本领。

禁止

医院里禁止吸烟。

湖边禁止钓鱼。

电影院里禁止大声喧哗(xuān huá)。

补充

野骆驼能让身体快速补充水分。

远洋轮船到港口补充水和食物。

近义词

难过——难受　　　　　　有趣——有意思

反义词

舒服——难受　　　　　　禁止——准许

多音字

jìn
禁
jìn
禁止

fèn
分
fèn
水分

jīn
禁
jīn
禁不住

fēn
分
fēn
分数

词语解释

境内——（国家的）边界以内。

荒凉——人烟稀少；冷清。

本领——技能；能力。

剧烈——猛烈。

捕食——抓住吃掉。

Lesson Five

The Wild Bactrian Camel

Almost everyone knows about the giant panda, yet few people know of the wild Bactrian camel. In fact, there are only about 800 wild camels left in the world, even less than the amount of pandas. They are rare and critically endangered animals.

The Wild Bactrian Camel Is Indigen

The record about camels can be dated back to the Han Dynasty in China and Li Shizhen of the Ming Dynasty mentioned both domestic and wild camels in the *Compendium of Materia Medica* (Pen-ts'ao Kan-mu), his masterpiece in pharmacology.

There are six types of camels in the world: guanaco, vicugna, llama, alpaca, dromedary and Bactrian camel, among which both guanaco and vicugna are wild, while llama, alpaca and dromedary are domestically bred now. Most Bactrian camels are domestic and only a small part of them remain to be wild and inhabit in Xinjiang, Gansu of China and in Mongolia.

Zoologists used to believe that all Bactrian camels had been domesticated and there was no wild species in the world. At the end of 19th century, the wild Bactrian camels were discovered in China's Xinjiang to the east of Lop Nur and to the north of the Altun Mountains. The discovery stirred the entire zoology community. In 1980, Chinese Academy of Sciences investigated Lop Nur and examined the wild Bactrian camels there. According to their research, the wild Bactrian camels living in China are protogenous wild species instead of the domestic camels going wild.

Vagabond in Desert

Among all rare wild animals living in China, the habitat of the wild camels is probably the harshest in the world. Their limited habitat is located in the driest desert of Central Asia, where the lowest temperature is 49 degree centigrade below zero and the highest temperature is 55 degree centigrade, the highest surface temperature there reaches 70 degree centigrade. This is a place without fresh water; the only drink is bitter and salty brine spring. There is no grass in most part of the area and sparse halogeton grows around brine pits. The wild camels live in this kind of environment, eating almost leafless plants and drinking saline water. They have no company except the sun, the moon, the wind and the sand.

It is not that the wild camels like to drink salt water; they have been forced into the nearly lifeless desert under heavy hunting pressure. The salt water bursting out of the ground serves as the only drink for the wild camels. It is a miracle that their livers slowly adapt to it; no other animals in the world have this ability and it is no easy job for the wild camels themselves, for many young camels under two years old die because their livers fail to accommodate to the cruel reality. Their physiology also changes greatly so as to survive in a harsh environment. A wild Bactrian camel can walk for two weeks in hot desert without drinking and its weight will reduce to three fourths of its original level. But when water is available, they can drink as much as 200 kilograms within several minutes and recover themselves at a miraculous speed. Zoologists believe that, for ordinary animals, the drastic changes of body water might probably endanger life itself. But as for the wild Bactrian camels, to quickly replenish body water is the secret for their survival in desert.

Through close observation, people find that a herd is usually composed of one male wild Bactrian camel, a dozen of female camels and their young camels. Males always fight for females and those who lose have to travel 150km to find other females. After the mating season, the males will also leave the herds; so during March and April, you might see some lonely wild Bactrian camels wander about. But they will not be too far away from their families and will rush back to protect the females and young camels in case of danger. Thirteen months later, female camels will also leave the herds to give birth to young camels.

Another interesting phenomenon about the wild camels is that they follow the same road to migrate as their ancestors did several hundred years ago. The footprints of the wild camels extend from one salt spring to another. When the plant around one spring is eaten up, they move to other place. Since they tend to travel along the same old road, you will see a path trod out by them extending to Altun Mountains. Every year, the wild camels will pass here to the shady valley of the Altun to avoid the summer heat in desert. In winter, they will come back to the central area of the desert.

It is mild in temperature during spring time, yet the wild camels have to deal with another danger, the desert storm, or the yellow and black sandstorm known to local people. The yellow sandstorm will block the sun and turn everything around golden yellow. The black sandstorm is even more frightful, for it will turn daytime into pitch black night, with sand and stones flying with the wind wildly. At this time, the poor camels can do nothing but lying down on the ground stretching their necks.

Another special skill the wild camels have is to cry. In fact, all camels shed tears and teardrops will stream down along their long eyelashes. Although we know that they cannot be happy living in sandstorm, yet they do not cry because they have a hard time there; they are using teardrops to wash away sand out of their eyes. Their nostrils are long and narrow, allowing them to breathe in sandstorms.

Saving the Wild Bactrian Camels

It is a miracle for such an ancient species as the wild Bactrian camels to survive in extremely harsh environment. Mother Nature grants us a precious species and what have we done to them?

Even today, the largest threat they have to deal with is still human beings. The local people used to hunt them for food. Though there are laws to protect wild animals and to ban the hunting of the wild Bactrian camels, the pastry area continuously expands, and the habitats of the wild Bactrian camels shrinks, making it more and more difficult for the wild camels to find food. These man-made disasters, together with natural disasters and natural enemies of wild wolves in mountains, result in the declining of its population, which declines from more than 10,000 some one hundred years ago to 2,000-3,000 in 1980's. Currently, there are only about 800 wild Bactrian camels in the world.

Up till now, there is almost no video film about the wild Bactrian camels and the pictures on them are also limited. In 1993, China distributed the first set of theme stamps on the wild Bactrian camels. It's our sincere hope that the stamps are not the only place that our descendents can see the wild Bactrian camels.

第六课

恒星真的不动吗?

"恒"字是持久不变的意思,难道恒星真的不动吗?为什么星座的形状看起来好像是固定不变的呢?

恒星并非静止不动,而是大动特动的。它们运动的速度,就连飞机、人造卫星、宇宙火箭也难赶上。更奇怪的是,恒星在天上运动,各有各的方向,有的向地球飞奔过来,有的离地球飞奔而去。恒星运动的速度也各不相同。

太阳系

你知道天狼星吗?它就以每秒8千米的速度朝地球方向奔来;织女星呢,速度比它快一些,每秒钟14千米;牛郎星的速度就更快了,每秒钟就有26千米。这不是比人造卫星、宇宙火箭快好几倍吗?既然恒星是动的,那为什么星座的形状不变呢?其实星座的形状也在变。我们熟知的北斗七星,十万年前、十万年后

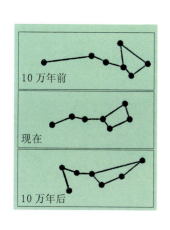

和现在的形状就都不一样。十万年才变动这么一些，往往就看不出变动了。不过这样的变动，用精密的测角仪器是完全可以测量出来的。8世纪初，有位叫一行的中国天文学家和几个人一起，制造了一台仪器叫黄道浑仪，用来测量星宿的经纬度。一行测量了许多星的位置，拿来与以前测量的结果比较，发现经度、纬度都变了，而且变动大小不一，有的变大，有的变小。从此以后，中国人就知道了恒星不是不动的，星宿的形状也不是不变的。一千年后，一位英国人也观察到了这个现象。

恒星动得那么快，速度甚至超过火箭，为什么我们看不出来呢？我们看到的快与慢，是和物体的远近有关系的。比如飞机在近处飞，我们看到的就是一掠而过，显得很快；若飞机在远处飞，我们就觉得慢腾腾的。不但如此，快慢还和运动方向有关，如果物体沿视线方向运动，速度再快，我们也不大感觉得出，看上去它总像是个点。恒星离我们非常遥远，而且有些恒星的运动方向正好是沿视线方向的，它们的移动也就看不出来了。因此，从地球上看去，恒星似乎就是不动的。

生词

héng xīng 恒星	fixed star	xiàn xiàng 现象	phenomenon
chí jiǔ 持久	permanent	shèn zhì 甚至	even
wèi xīng 卫星	satellite	chāo guò 超过	surpass, go above
huǒ jiàn 火箭	rocket	wù tǐ 物体	object
jīng mì 精密	precise	guān xì 关系	relation
yí qì 仪器	instrument	yí lüè ér guò 一掠而过	swiftly
jīng dù 经度	longitude	màn tēng tēng 慢腾腾	slowly
wěi dù 纬度	latitude	shì xiàn 视线	line of vision

听写

持久　精密　仪器　甚至　超过　慢腾腾　视线

移动　关系　现象　＊纬度　恒星

比一比

视 { 电视 / 视线 }　　恒 { 恒星 / 永恒 }　　超 { 超过 / 超级市场 }

字词运用

甚至

他虽然是美国人,但是中文讲得不错,甚至还会唱京剧呢!

儿子已经长得很高,甚至超过了爸爸。

测验　测量

每次上中文课几乎都有小测验。

这块地有多大,只要测量一下就知道了。

反义词

静止——运动　　　　　固定——移动

多音字

系 xì　　　　　系 jì
关系 xì　　　　系上 jì

词语解释

移动——改换原来的位置。

相配词语连线

熟练的　　　矿藏

坚强的　　　变化

扩大　　　　环境

有趣的　　　范围

剧烈的　　　技巧

开采　　　　意志

保护　　　　故事

阅读

只有一个地球

飞上太空的宇航员说，他们在天空看到的地球，是一个晶莹(yíng)明亮的球体，周围包着一层薄薄的水蓝色"纱衣"。

地球，这位人类的母亲，这个生命的摇篮，是那么美丽可亲。但是，地球又是一个半径只有6300多千米的星球，在茫茫宇宙中，就像一叶扁舟。

地球不大，而人类生活的陆地只占其中的1/5。也就是说人类活动的范围本来就不大。

地球的自然资源也是有限的。拿矿产资源来说，那是经过几百万年，甚至几亿年的地质变化才形成的。如果毫无计划地乱挖乱采，总有一天会把资源用完的。

人类生活所需要的水资源、森林资源、生物资源、大气资源本来是可以不断再生，长期为人类服务的，但是由于人们随意破坏自然，滥用化学品，致使它们不能再生。

有人会说宇宙无边无际，那里有数不清的星球，我们能不能搬到别的星球上去？不错，科学家们提出了许多设想，例如：在火星或者月球上建造移民村。但是，目前看来，这些设想能不能实现还说不准，即使能实现，也是遥远的将来的事情。科学家已经证明，至少在以地球为中心的40万亿千米之内，没有适合人类居住的第二个星球。人类不能指望在破坏了地球以后，再移居到别的星球上去。

"我们这个地球太可爱了，同时又太容易被破坏了！"这是宇航员发出的感叹。只有一个地球，如果它被破坏了，我们别无去处。我们要精心地保护地球，保护地球的生态环境。让地球更好地造福子孙后代！

Lesson Six

Are Fixed Stars Really Fixed?

The word "fixed" means permanence and no change, is it true that the fixed starts are really fixed and do not move? Why do the constellations remain the same all the time?

The fixed stars are not fixed, on the contrary, they move about a lot at a high speed and no airplane, man-made satellite or space rocket can catch up with them. Another interesting thing about the stars is that they move at different speed in different directions; some rush toward the earth and some fly away from the earth.

Have you ever seen the Canicula? It rushes toward the earth at the speed of 8 kilometers per second. The Vega moves faster at 14 kilometers per second and the Altair flies even faster at 26 kilometers per second, which is several times faster than both man-made satellites and space rockets. If the fixed stars move, then why do their shapes remain the same? Actually, the shapes of constellations also change. The Big Dipper that is familiar to all of us was not the same as we see today one hundred thousand years ago and one hundred thousand years later. Since its shape changes only a little bit during one hundred thousand years, its shape seems to be fixed for us. But its change can be measured with precisely designed angular instrument. At the beginning of the 8th century, Chinese astronomer Yixing and his fellows devised an ecliptic armillary sphere to measure the latitude and longitude of stars. Yixing compared the locations of many stars he measured with those measured before and found that both their latitude and longitude have changed. He also found that the range of variation was also different. Since then, Chinese have known that the fixed stars were not fixed and that the shape of constellation didn't remain the same over years. One thousand years later, an Englishman also noticed the fact through observation.

If the stars move at such a high speed and even faster than the rockets, then why is it that we can't see? Both swiftness and slowness we see are actually relative concepts and closely related to the distance. For example, when a plane flies by close to you, its speed is very high; but a plane flying at distance might appear to you slow. More than that, the speed also relates to the direction of movement; an object moving at a high speed along the direction of your vision line looks like a dot. Since the stars are far away from us and some stars move along the direction of our vision, we can't see their movement so the stars appear to us motionless looked from the earth.

We Have Only One Earth

The astronauts traveling to the outer space said that the earth they saw from the space was a bright and translucent globe wrapped in a thin layer of light blue gauze.

The earth is our Mother and the cradle of life; it is so beautiful and affable. Yet at the same time, the earth is a planet whose radius is only 6,300 kilometers, a small boat in the vast sea of the universe.

The earth is not big, on which one fifth inhabited with human beings, whose sphere of activity is accordingly very limited.

The natural resources on earth are also limited. Taking mineral resources as example, they are formed during millions of years or even hundreds of millions of years through geologic changes. The earth provides resources to human beings, yet the unplanned exploitation results in increasingly shrinking mineral resources on the earth.

The basic elements for human life, including water resources, forest resources, biological resources and air resource, used to be renewable resources and to serve the mankind for a long period of time. But since people destroy the natural resources at will and abuse chemical products, they are now no longer regenerated.

Some will say that the universe is vast with numerous stars and why can't we move to another planet? It is true that scientists propose many solutions, such as to construct an immigrant base on the Mars or on the moon. But, as matters stand, even these plans are realized, that will be in the far-away future. The scientists have already proved that there is no planet that is suitable for human beings to live on except the earth within an area of 4,000 billion kilometers centering on the earth. We just cannot count on moving to another planet after destroying the earth.

The astronaut sighed at the sight of the earth from the outer space: "Our planet is so beautiful and at the same time so vulnerable." We have only one earth and will have no other place to go if we destroy it. We should take special care of the earth, should protect its ecological environment and allow the earth to bring benefit to our descendents.

第七课

灰尘的旅行

　　灰尘是地球上永不疲倦的旅行者，它随着空气的流动而飘荡。我们周围的空气，从室内到室外，从城市到郊野，从平地到高山，从沙漠到海洋，几乎处处都有灰尘。真正没有灰尘的空间，只有实验室里才能制造出来。

　　在晴朗的天空下，灰尘是看不见的，只有阳光穿过百叶窗射进黑暗的房间时，才能够清楚地看到无数的灰尘在空中飞舞。大的灰尘肉眼可以看见，小的灰尘比细菌还小，用显微镜也看不到。在干燥的日子里，城市街道上的空气，每一立方厘米大约有10万粒以上的灰尘；在海洋上空的空气里，每一立方厘米大约有1000多粒灰尘；在野外和高山的空气里，每一立方厘米只有几十粒灰尘；在住宅区的空气里，灰尘要比海洋和野外多得多。

　　这样多的灰尘在空中游荡着，对气象的变化产生了不少的影响。原来灰尘还是制造云雾和雨点的小工程师。它们会帮助空气中的水分凝结成云雾和雨点。没有它们，就没有白云在天空飘动，也没有大雨和小雨了。没有它们，夏天强烈的日光会直接照射在大地上，使气温不能降低。这是灰尘在自然界的作用。如果

我们追问一下，灰尘到底是些什么东西呢？它们是从什么地方来的？回答是：有的是来自山地岩石的碎屑，有的是来自田野的土末，有的是来自海面上浪花蒸发后生成的食盐粉末，有的是来自火山灰，还有的是来自星际空间的宇宙尘。这些都是天然的灰尘。

还有人工的灰尘，主要是来自烟囱的烟尘和水泥厂、化工厂、纺织工厂、面粉工厂等地的灰尘。除了这些无机灰尘以外，还有有机灰尘。有机的灰尘，如花粉、棉絮、种子、毛发、虫卵等，还有各种细菌、病毒和人畜的粪便。许多灰尘对人类生活是有害的。自从有机物参加到灰尘的队伍以来，这种危害性就更加严重了。

灰尘的旅行，对于人类的生活有什么害处呢？它们不但把我

们的空气弄脏，还会弄脏我们的房屋、家具、衣服，以及手和脸的皮肤。它们落到机器里，会使机器的光滑部分磨坏；它们会毁坏我们的工业品，把它们变成废品。这些还是小事，灰尘里面还夹杂着病菌和病毒，它们是人类健康的最危险的敌人。

灰尘是呼吸道的破坏者，它们会使鼻孔不通，气管发炎，引起伤风、感冒、肺炎等病。此外，金属的粉末，特别是铅，会使人中毒；石灰和水泥的粉尘，会伤害我们的肺和皮肤。当遇到这些有害的粉末和灰尘时，为了安全，我们必须戴上面具或口罩。最后，粉尘还会引起爆炸，这是严重的事故，必须加以防止。

因此，不能让灰尘乱飞乱跑。我们要让洒水汽车在街道上洒水，把城市和工业区变成花园，让每一个工厂都能通风和吸尘。近年来，人类正在努力控制灰尘的旅行，使它不再成为祸害，而为我们的利益服务。

（本文根据高士其《灰尘的旅行》改编）

中文科普阅读

生词

huī chén 灰尘	dust		huǐ huài 毁坏	destroy
pí juàn 疲倦	tired		fèi pǐn 废品	waste product
qíng lǎng 晴朗	sunny		fèi yán 肺炎	pneumonia
xiǎn wēi jìng 显微镜	microscope		jīn shǔ 金属	metal
lí mǐ 厘米	centimeter		qiān 铅	lead
níng jié 凝结	condense		kǒu zhào 口罩	gauze mask
zuò yòng 作用	effect; function		shì gù 事故	accident
suì xiè 碎屑	scrap		fáng zhǐ 防止	prevent; avoid
zhēng fā 蒸发	evaporate		sǎ shuǐ 洒水	sprinkle water
fěn mò 粉末	powder		lì yì 利益	interest; benefit
yān cōng 烟囱	chimney		fú wù 服务	serve

听写

灰尘　防止　晴朗　细菌　废品　事故　铅

服务　肺炎　洒水　*烟囱　疲倦

比一比

郊 { 郊野 / 郊区 }　　朗 { 晴朗 / 朗诵 }　　市 { 城市 / 市场 }　　{ 废（废品） / 费（花费） }

菌 { 细菌 / 病菌 }　　镜 { 眼镜 / 显微镜 }　　{ 凝（凝结） / 疑（怀疑） }　　{ 洒（洒水） / 酒（饮酒） }

字词运用

实验室　真实　其实　事实

学生们在生物实验室里做实验。

有的报纸上的新闻并不完全真实。

做了错事其实并不可怕，可怕的是不承认错误。

我们应该承认篮球比赛输给了他们这个事实。

吸烟　冒烟

医院里禁止吸烟。

远处的山林大火，冒着黑烟。

严重

她的病很严重。

这是一起严重的事故。

洒　撒

扫地以前先在地上洒点水吧，不然就会尘土飞扬。

一不小心，我把薯条撒了一地。

跳舞　飞舞

每个星期六小乔都要去学跳舞。

刮大风了，尘土满天飞舞。

防止

开车不闯红灯，可以防止交通事故。

为了防止中毒，小孩子不要自己采蘑菇吃。

近义词

疲倦——疲劳　　　　　郊野——郊外

毁坏——破坏　　　　　作用——影响

词语解释

灰尘——尘土。

者——（助词）一般指人，如：旅行者、受害者、胜利者。

郊野——城市外面的田野或空地。

面具——戴在面部遮挡和保护脸的东西。

云 和 雨

我们周围的空气中总含有一些水。你看不到空气中有水,是因为水成为蒸气了。你也感觉不出空气中有水,因为水蒸气并不湿。有人以为雾就是水蒸气,那就错了。雾其实是无数细微的水滴。水进入空气只能靠蒸发。水从湖面上、海面上蒸发,也从地面上蒸发。水从晾着的湿衣服上蒸发,也从花草树木上蒸发。你信不信?在夏天的烈日下,20棵玉米一天能蒸发大约1吨(dūn)水。我们的皮肤出汗,水就从我们身上蒸发了。只要有水的地方,或是含水分的东西,差不多都有水在蒸发,因而我们总是被水蒸气包围着,直到空气里的水蒸气已经足够多,水的蒸发才会停止。那时候,衣服难以晒干,人们身上也总是湿漉(lù)漉的。因为汗水也停止了蒸发。人们呼吸很不舒畅(chàng),会说:"这天气真闷(mēn)热!"

我们知道,靠近地面的空气总是比较热,热空气含水蒸气多,因此也比较轻。轻的气体会往上升。可是离地面越远,气温越低,上升的空气受了冷,它所含的水蒸气就会被挤出,凝结成细微的水滴,这种空中的雾就是云。可是有的云不是由水滴,而是由细小的冰晶组成的。水蒸气在空中凝结,可以成为水滴,也可以成为冰晶,得看凝结时的温度是在冰点以上,还是在冰点以下。

我们看云,云是各式各样的,最常见的有三种。

第一种云像马尾,又像羽毛,叫做"卷云"。天晴时,天空中常有这种云出现。卷云很高,大概在离地面一万几千米的高空中,是由细小的冰晶组成的。高空中风很大,因而卷云飞得很快,几乎跟最快的飞机一样快。只是因为它高,我们在地面上看并不觉得它在飘动。

第二种云好像一座一座的山,叫做"积云"。天空中有这种云,常常是好天气。但是积云如果越积越多,变得又黑又大,会成为"雷云",一场大雷雨就快来了。积云比卷云低得多,云脚离地面一般只有两千米。成为雷云的时候,它可能有七八千米厚。

第三种云叫做"层云"。层云常常铺满整个天空,成为灰色,不很厚,也不很高。在天空布满层云的日子,如果你站在高山顶上,你仍然可以看到明亮的太阳,而层云在你脚下好像波涛起伏的大海。

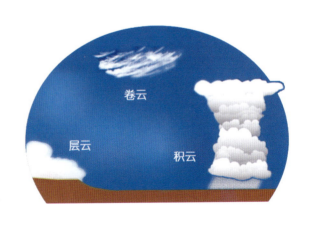

含水蒸气多的空气要是很快地升到高空中,大部分就凝结

成较大的水滴，于是下起雨来。落下来的水滴在途中又合并别的水滴，变得更大。雨滴至少比组成云的水滴大上几百万倍。

雨下得多少，通常用毫米来计算。6000米厚的一片云完全变成雨，落到地上的雨水还不到10毫米。这个数量看起来很小，其实并不小。如果100平方米的地面落下10毫米的雨水，雨水的总重量就有1吨。有时一场暴雨，1小时内可以下250毫米。因而在山区连下几个小时暴雨，常常会引起山洪、泥石流，冲毁村庄、桥梁、公路或者铁路。

Lesson Seven

Journey of Dust

  Dust is a never tired traveler on the earth and drifts about along with the movement of air. Dust is almost everywhere in the air surrounding us, from downtown areas to suburbs, from plains to high mountains, and from deserts to oceans. The dustless space can only be created in laboratories.

  We cannot see dust under the fine sky. But if you stay in a dark room, allowing sunshine illuminates it through the window shutter, you will then clearly see much dust dancing in the air. Bigger dust particles are visible to eyes, yet the small ones are smaller than bacteria and cannot be seen even with the help of the microscope. During dry days, there are more than 100,000 dust particles in the air of one cubic centimeter above the city streets. In the air above the ocean, the amount reduces to 1,000; while in the open air and high mountains, the amount further reduces to dozens of dust particles per cubic centimeter. The dust density in the air of residential area is much higher than both ocean and outdoors.

  So many dust particles floating in the air greatly affect the meteorologic changes and it turns out that dust particles are little engineers producing cloud, mist and rain. They help the moisture in the air to condense into cloud, mist and raindrops. Without them, there will be no white clouds in the sky, no shower or drizzle; without them, summer sun will shine directly on the earth and the temperature will be very high.

These are the main functions of dust in nature. If we examine it further, we might ask: where does dust come from and what is it? The answer is: part of it comes from the fines of mountainous rocks, part of it comes from the mud powder of the field, part of it comes from salt powder produced after the sea water evaporates, part of it comes from volcanic ash, and part of it comes from cosmic dust of interstellar space. This is natural dust.

There is also man-made dust, which is mainly composed of chimney soot and dust from cement mills, chemical plants, textile factories and flour mills. Apart from inorganic dust, there is organic dust including pollen, cotton fiber, seeds, hairs, ova, and various kinds of bacteria and virus as well as night soil produced by human beings and livestock. Many types of dust are harmful to human beings and since the joining of organic dust, the hazardness of dust increases.

What kind of harm does traveling dust do to our lives? It not only pollutes our air, but also smudges our houses, furniture, clothing, and skin of our hands and face. If it falls into a machine, it will make smooth parts of the machine abrade; and it will destroy our industrial products and turn them into wastes. If all these seem insignificant, then the bacteria and virus carried in dust are the most dangerous enemies to our health.

Dust is a destroyer of our respiratory system and will result in a stuffy nose, trachea inflammation and lead into such diseases of cold, flu or pneumonia. In addition, metal powder, especially lead, is poisonous; lime and cement powders do harm to both our lungs and skin. Therefore, when we are in the poisonous powder and dust, we must wear face masks or gauze masks for the sake of safeness. On top of it, metal powder might cause explosion and this is a serious accident that should be prevented.

Therefore, we shall not allow dust travel freely. We should use sprinkler trucks to sprinkle water on the road, turn cities and industrial zones into parks, make all factories well-ventilated and dust-controlled. In recent years, people try their best to control the journey of dust, guaranteeing that it does no harm to human beings and serves our interests instead.

Adapted from *Journey of Dust* by Gao Shiqi

Cloud and Rain

The air surrounding us always contains water, but you cannot see it, for it is in the form of vapor; neither can you feel it, for it is not wet. Some might take fog or mist as vapor; in fact, it is not. Mist is actually composed of numerous fine water drops. The only way that water goes into air is evaporation. Water evaporates from the surface of rivers, lakes and oceans as well as from the ground. It evaporates from wet clothes dried by airing and from trees, flowers and grass as well. Believe it or not, during a hot summer day, the water evaporating from 20 corn plants weighs about one metric ton. Water also evaporates from our bodies in the form of sweat through skins. Wherever there is water or objects containing water, there is evaporation. Therefore, we are always surrounded by vapor. When there is enough vapor

in the air, the evaporation will stop. When this occurs, it is difficult for the clothes to be dried by airing and people's skin is wet, for sweat also stops vaporizing. People will feel difficult to breathe and will say: "it's stuffy today."

We know the air close to the ground is relatively high in temperature, contains more vapor and is accordingly relatively lighter. Lighter air rises and the higher it goes, the lower its temperature. When rising hot air meets cold air, part of the vapor it contains will condense into fine water drops. This kind of fog in air is cloud. Some clouds are composed of fine icy particles instead of water drops. Vapor in air might condense into either water drops or icy particles, depending on the fact that the condensation temperature is above or below freezing point.

When we look at the clouds in the sky, we can see that they are in different shapes and there are three main types of clouds.

The first one looks like horse tail or feather and is called "cirrus." After it becomes fine, the clouds in the sky are most likely cirrus. This kind of cloud is usually high in the sky of more than ten thousand meters high and is composed of fine ice particles. Since the wind in the high sky is strong, cirrus flies at a high speed and is as fast as the plane at its highest speed. It is because cirrus is high that people standing on the ground barely notice its movement.

The second most commonly seen cloud looks like mountain ranges and is named "cumulus." It usually appears in the afternoon sky of summer and indicates good weather. But when it gradually accumulates and becomes dark and large, it will turn into the thunder cloud, indicating that a big storm is coming. Cumulus is much lower than cirrus and its bottom line is usually only 2,000 meters above ground. When it becomes thunder cloud, it will be 7,000-8,000 meters thick.

The third common cloud is "stratus" and usually covers the entire sky, making it grey in color. It is not thick and not high. When the sky is covered with stratus, people standing at a high peak might still see blue sky and shiny sun, while the clouds surge like sea below their feet.

When the air with much vapor rises into the sky quickly, most of it will condense into relatively large water drops and it will then rain. The falling rain drops might also merge with other water drops during the process of falling down and thus make the rain heavier. The rain drops are at least several million times bigger than the water drops consisting clouds.

Rainfall is usually measured in the unit of millimeter. If a pile of clouds of 6,000 meters thick turns into rain and reach the ground, the rainfall will be no more than 10 millimeters. The figure is not as small as it looks, since if the rainfall is measured in an area of 100 square meters, then the total weight of the rain will reach one metric ton. Sometimes, the rainfall of a one-hour storm will reach 250 millimeters; so a storm lasting several hours in mountainous area might cause flash flood and result in mudrock flow, destroying the farmland, villages, bridges, roads and railways.

第八课

盐井和井盐

屋子里的深井

盐井是一口井吗?当然是一口井。那么,盐井跟水井有什么不一样呢?水井里的水是淡的;盐井里的水是咸的,水里含有盐。盐井和水井难道只有这个区别吗? 不,不同的地方多着呢!请听我慢慢地讲。

四川自贡盐井

水井大多在露天,盐井却全在屋子里。水井的井口有洗澡盆那么大,盐井的却只有汤盆口粗细。水井,最深的也就是一二十米;盐井却深得惊人,最浅的也有300米,深的有近千米呢!而且最惊人的是那千米深的盐井,完全是人工凿成的。

据说汲井水熬盐的方法是战国时期秦国人李冰发明的。传说不足全信,但是我们至少可以认定,在两千多年前,四川已经开凿盐井了。在汉朝留下来的砖上就有汲水熬盐的图。

挖盐井，第一件事是请个有经验的人，找到可以打出盐水的地方。然后，跟凿水井一样，挖个大坑。挖不了多深，泥层就到了底，下面是石块。石工便下到坑底，接着往下凿石。凿到十多米深处时，坑口很容易倒塌，需要用石圈垒起来，挡住周围的泥土和不坚固的岩石。石圈是用很大的石块凿成的。从10米深的坑底，一个个往上垒，石圈垒上十来个，就跟地面齐平了。石圈的窟窿只有大汤盆的盆口大小，也就是说，石圈里面的直径在30厘米左右。不是还要往深挖吗？当然还要往下挖，上千米的深井，这才开了个头呢。既然井口只有大汤盆的盆口粗细，再挖，工人怎么下得去呢？工人不再下井了，从此，他们在地面上工作。

大钻头和大钻机

钻头和钻机是钢做的，钻头有200多种，有的还带着倒_{dào}钩；木把_{bà}是用最结实的木头做的。

钻机是一个很大很大的转轮，工人叫它"大盘车"，它的直径为5米~7米。石圈垒好了，工人就把大盘车架在井口边。这盘车的作用和水井上的辘_{lù}轳_{lu}一样，以后汲取盐水，全凭它了；眼前要往下挖井，也全靠着它。对了，还得用绳子，用一条奇怪的绳子。工人们把一些宽7厘米左右的竹片，一片一片地接起来，需要多长，他们就做成多长的竹片绳子。

舂了一下又一下

工人把竹片绳子绕在盘车上，钻头捆在竹片绳子的一头，从石圈中直沉到井底。于是，工人一来一往地推动盘车，竹片绳子一提一放，钻头就一下一下地往下凿。实际上不是凿，只是一下一下地舂。钻头非常重，就靠那重量把岩石给舂碎。地下多少有点儿水，舂下来的石屑，跟水和(huò)成了泥浆，要像以后汲盐水一样，把它汲出来。就这样一下一下，5年，10年，20年……直凿到井底冒出盐水来。到底要凿多久呢？"那得看运气。"凿井的工人全这么说。

熬盐

没有底儿的水桶

井底冒出盐水来了。可是井那么深，用什么方法才能把井底的盐水汲上来？"那很简单，用个水桶……"

你忘记了，井口只有大汤盆口粗细，一般的水桶是下不去的。从盐井里汲水，有一种专用的水桶。那水桶又细又长，是把两根到四根打通了节的粗竹竿连起来做成的。更奇怪的是，那么长的水桶并没有底儿。没有底儿，那怎么盛得了水呢？原来，在那个长水桶的下面，有一块牛皮做的圆形的活板。水桶到了井底，往盐水里一插，盐水就把活板冲开，进到了水桶里。等到往上提水桶的时候，桶里的盐水就会压住活板，流不出来了。水桶提到了地面上，用不着把它横过来，只要用个铁钩把活板向上一顶，盐水就哗哗地流出来了。"这方法真妙。"是的，有的水桶一二十米长，要让它不倒下来，可不太容易。所以每个盐井上都有个高高的木架子。木架子中间有个又细又长的竹笼。水桶从井里升起来，穿进那竹笼，就不会倒下来了。到了盐井集中的地方，可以看见许多高高的木架子像森林一样，每个木架子下面就是一口盐井。

把水桶提起来，也得用盘车。用一条牛、两条牛，甚至三条牛拉着盘车转上四五十圈，才能把一桶盐水从井底提到地面上。盐水汲出来，就可以熬盐了。因为盘车和盐井全在屋子里面，所以生产不受天气的影响。一般来说，一天一夜才能出一次盐。

盐井　选自《天工开物》

日夜不熄的火

从井里汲上来的盐水又黄又浊，过滤之后，放到锅里。锅下面的火日夜不熄灭，火上面是成排的锅，工人不断地搅动锅里的盐水。等到水分慢慢地蒸发干了，锅里就结出了一颗颗洁白的盐粒。这就是井盐。

在古代，贸易极不发达、交通极不便利的情况下，生活在内陆地区的人们，就是用这种方法获得了宝贵的盐。

生 词

盐井 yán jǐng	salt	竹竿 zhú gān	bamboo pole
区别 qū bié	difference	哗哗 huā huā	clang
露天 lù tiān	open air	熬 áo	extract by long heating
汲水 jí shuǐ	draw water	影响 yǐng xiǎng	affect
倒塌 dǎo tā	collapse	过滤 guò lǜ	filtrate
(圆)圈 yuán quān	circle	熄灭 xī miè	extinguish; put out
窟窿 kū long	hole	搅动 jiǎo dòng	stir
直径 zhí jìng	diameter	获得 huò dé	get
捆 kǔn	bind; bundle up	能干 néng gàn	able; capable

听写

盐井　露天　直径　影响　获得　圆圈　能干

捆　区别　竹竿　*熄灭　倒塌

比一比

钢（钢铁）　锅（饭锅）　竿（竹竿）　　　泥浆
刚（刚才）　祸（车祸）　杆（一杆秤）　浆　纸浆

熄（熄火）　钩（铁钩）　捆（捆上）　　　至少
息（休息）　沟（水沟）　困（困难）　至　至今

字词运用

露天　露水

公园里有个露天音乐厅。

清晨，草地上满是露水。

窟窿

弟弟的裤子上总是磨出窟窿。

田地里有一些窟窿，可能是田鼠的洞。

直径

草原上的蒙古包直径只有4米左右。

影响

上课不举手就说话，会影响别人听讲。

晚上熬夜，会影响身体健康。

能干

我爸爸很能干，他不但会修自行车，还会修汽车。

近义词

结实——牢固　　　凭——靠　　　捆——扎

多音字

zuān
钻
zuān
钻进去

zuàn
钻
zuàn
钻头

shèng
盛
shèng
盛大

chéng
盛
chéng
盛水

概数的表达

三十厘米左右　　一百个上下　　十来个　　大约五六个

大概二三十人　　十七八个　　二百多斤　　将近一千人

阅读

电影的生日

1895年12月28日，星期六。

这一天下午，法国巴黎(lí)的许多记者、剧院经理、科学家和社会名流，手里拿着粉红色的请帖，来到一家"大咖(kā fēi)啡馆"的地下室。这地下室不算太大。来宾们一走进去，只见除了一排排的椅子之外，墙上还挂着一块白布。

"叫我们这么老远跑来看一块白布，太没意思了。"人们议论着。忽然咖啡馆的灯熄灭了，一片黑暗。白布上出现了奇迹：一道光照在白布上，人们看到了街上的情景，看到了火车站，看到了工厂的大门，看到了许多人在白布上跑来跑去……那些刚才还大叫没意思的人，一下子目瞪口呆说不出话来。一位记者曾这样报道当时的情形："一辆马车被飞跑的马拉着，迎面跑来。我邻座中一位女士看到这景象时，害怕得突然站了起来，一直等到那辆车子转过去不见了，她才重新坐下来。"据说，有的人看到火车飞奔而来，吓得拔腿就跑，不小心踩痛了别人的脚，两个人大吵起来；还有的人看见白布上下起大雨，赶紧打起了雨伞！人们在看什么呢？原来，人们正在观看一种从未见过的艺术——电影！

这天下午放了第一场电影之后，消息很快就传开了。第二天就有许多人排队买电影票。于是这家咖啡馆门口热闹起来，每天上演20多场电影。从此，电影开始在全世界风行起来。

早期的一部影片叫《火车到站》，拍摄的是一辆火车开进车站，旅客们上上下下，然后火车开走了，影片也就演完了，内容十分简单。还有一部电影名叫《婴(yīng)儿喝汤》，演的是婴儿喝汤。汤喝光了，电影也就结束了。当时最受欢迎的影片是《水浇园丁》，因为它有一点情节：园丁正用胶皮管浇水，一个调皮的孩子偷偷用脚踩住了胶皮管，园丁只好拿起胶皮管检查，这时，孩子一抬脚，水突然从胶皮管里喷出，浇得园丁满脸是水。影片就在观众的哄(hōng)堂大笑中结束了。

由于电影是在1895年12月28日这一天诞生的，这一天就被定为电影的生日。

（根据叶永烈《电影》改编）

Lesson Eight

Brine Well and Well Salt

Deep Well inside House

Is a brine well a well too? Sure it is. Then what's the difference between a salt well and normal water well? The water in water well is fresh and nonsaline, while that in brine well is salty. Is this the only difference? There are many differences and I'll talk about them one by one.

Most water wells are in the open air, but all brine wells are in houses. The mouth of the water well is as big as a bathing basin, yet that of the salt well is only as big as a soup plate. Most water wells are ten to twenty meters in depth while brine wells are astonishingly deep with the shallow ones of 300 meters and deep ones are nearly 1,000 meters underground. The most incredible thing about it is that the 1,000 meter deep well is dug with hands.

It is said that the method of boiling brine well water for salt can be traced back to Li Bing of the Qing State of the Warring States Period. The hearsay is not totally credible, but we can be sure with at least one thing: More than two thousand years ago, people began to dig salt wells in Sichuan Province, for there is pictures about taking and boiling well water for salt painted on the ancient bricks of Han Dynasty.

Before digging a salt well, the first task is to invite an experienced person to decide on the place of digging. Then people begin to dig a large pit as digging water well until they reach the bottom of mud layer and then rock layer. Stone masons go to the bottom of the pit and chisel through the rock. When the well is about ten meters deep, the pit mouth tends to collapse and needs to be supported with stone rings, which can fence off surrounding mud and loose rocks. The stone rings are carved out of big stone blocks. Starting from the bottom of 10-meter pit, workers lay a dozen of stone rings upward one by one till ground level. The hole at the center of the stone rings is the size of a plate bowl with about 30 centimeter in diameter. "Are they going to dig further?" Sure enough; this is just the beginning of a 1,000-meter deep well. "Then how could it possible for workers to work on it since the well mouth is only the size of a soup plate?" They won't get into the well to work; instead, they will work outside the well on the ground.

Big Drilling Bit and Large Drilling Machine

Both drilling bit and drilling machine are made of steel and there are more than 200 types of drilling bits, some of which have barbs. The handles are all made of the most solid wood.

The drilling machine is a very large rotating wheel, which the workers call "big turning machine." It is 5-7 meters in diameter. After all the stone rings are laid, workers will erect the big turning machine at the well mouth. The machine functions as a winch besides a water well; it can be used to dig well now and draw salt water from the well later. Another important thing is a rope and the rope they use is strange and no ordinary. The workers connect bamboo strips of 7 centimeter in width until satisfactory length they need.

Pounding at the Bottom of the Well

Workers wind the bamboo rope around the big wheel and attach the drilling pit at one end of the rope, lowering it through the hole into the bottom of the well. They then rotate the wheel to raise and lower the rope made of bamboo strips, and the drilling pit will chisel at the rock at the bottom of the well. This is actually pounding instead of chiseling, for the drilling bit is heavy and this helps to pound the rock into small pieces. Since there is water underground, the stone chips smashed mix with water and become mud, which can be drawn out as they draw salt water later. Just like that, one pounding after another, five years, ten years, or twenty years… until there is salt water emitting out of the well bottom. How long does it take? "It's a matter of sheer luck," almost all well diggers will say so.

Bucket without Bottom

So there is salt water emitting, but it is such a deep well and how can people draw salt water out of it? "That's simple, use a bucket…"

But you forget it is a well whose mouth is only the size of a soup plate and no ordinary water bucket can go through it. There is a special bucket for drawing water from a salt well. The bucket is thin and deep, made of two to four thick bamboo poles with joints cut through. The most interesting thing about the bucket is that it has no bottom. "How can a bucket without bottom hold water?" It turns out that there is a round loose plate made of cattle hide at the bottom of the long bucket. When the bucket reaches the bottom of the well and is put into salt water, the water will break through the loose plate and enter the bucket. When people bring up the bucket, the water inside it will press against the plate without outflow. When the bucket is carried out, you don't have to tip it; instead, a pushing up of the loose plate with an iron hook will allow all salt water inside to flow out. "What a clever design," you might say. Yes, indeed. Since some buckets are ten to twenty meters long, it is difficult for them to keep upright without falling down. Therefore, there is a high wood stand over each salt well and a thin and long cylinder constructed of bamboo is hung in the middle of it. The bucket is drawn out of the well and then went into the cylinder to avoid falling down. In a place where there are many salt wells, the high wood supporters standing over them remind people of the forest and there is one salt well below each wood supporter.

People use the wheel machine to draw the bucket and the machine is usually driven by cattle, one, two or three of them at a time. They have to rotate forth or fifty rounds of the wheel in order to draw one bucket of salt water from the bottom to the ground. Since both the wheel and the well are inside houses, the production is not affected by weather. After the salt water is drawn, the process of boiling salt can then begin. Generally, the salt can be boiled out after one day and one night.

The Fire Burning Day and Night

The salt water drawn from wells is yellowish and opaque. It is pour into pots after being filtrated. The fire under the pots burns day and night and the pots are arranged in a row; workers must stir the salt water regularly. Then the water will evaporate and white salt appears in pots. This is well salt.

In ancient China featuring undeveloped trade and extremely inconvenient transport, our ancestors living in inland areas got the much-needed salt in this method. Aren't they hard-working, industrious, intelligent and able people?

The Birthday of Movie

It was a Saturday on 28 December, 1895.

On the afternoon of that day, many journalists, theater managers, scientists and celebrities in Paris, France, went to the basement of the Grand Café with pink invitations. The basement was not a large one and the guests saw a piece of white cloth hung on a wall besides rows of chairs in it.

"It was meaningless to ask us travel such a long way here to see just a piece of white cloth." As people discussed, the lights were out and it was dark inside the coffee shop. Something miraculous happened to the white cloth: a beam of light was projected onto the cloth and the viewers saw their familiar street scenes including the railway station, the factory entrance and many people running around on the white cloth… Those who shouted it was meaningless just now became speechless instantly. One journalist reported the event later: "A carriage driven by flying horses ran right toward you. At this scene, a female viewer besides me was so frightened that she stood up suddenly and waited until the carriage turned around the corner out of sight before sitting down again." It is said that someone saw a train running toward the audience and started running at once, stepped on someone else's foot and they had a quarrel. Some others hurriedly open their umbrellas once it began to rain on the white cloth. What were they doing and looking at? It turns out that they were appreciating a new art form: movie.

Since the afternoon when the fist public show was made, the message has been spread out quickly. In the following day, many people queued for movie tickets and the entrance of the coffee shop became a crowded place. There were more than twenty shows each day and movie became popular in the world.

One of the first movies is *A Train Pulling into Station*, which describes how a train pulls into station, how passengers get on and off the train. At last, the train leaves and the film ends. The plot is very simple. Another movie is *Feeding a Baby with Soup*, shooting how a baby eats soup and the film ends at the baby finishing soup. The most popular movie at the time is *Watering the Gardener*, for it tells a story. A gardener is watering with a plastic hose and a naughty kid steps on the hose stealthily. When the gardener holds the hose to check it, water bursts out of the hose and sprinkles the face of the gardener instead after the child lifted the foot up. The movie ends among the laughter of the audience.

The day of 28 December 1895 has ever since been regarded as the birthday of movie.

Adapted from *The Movie* by Ye Yongle

第九课

我们应该长多高

大自然创造出了人类，人类的体形比起鲸、大象，当然矮小；比起昆虫、田鼠，却又如此高大。人类就这样存在于大自然规定的尺寸之中。

从1.5米到2米，这大约是地球上几十亿男男女女的身高范围。吉尼斯世界大全上，身高2.27米的美国男子和身高0.48米的荷兰女子，恐怕可以算是目前世界人类身高的上限和下限了。

人们往往认为，高大意味着健康、强壮、力量和俊美，然而，我们有没有认真考虑过，人类究竟应该长多高才好呢？先扯点不相关的事，也许有助于我们打开思路。这是一块普通的豆腐，它很好地保持着自身的形体。但如果把它做得大些，再大些，将会出现什么情景呢？瞧，豆腐垮了！这个试验好像对大个子不利。那么，是否豆腐强度太弱，不能说明什么问题呢？

我们再以岩石为例。一座石头山，能够无限增高吗？计算表明，在地球上，山的高度不能超过11,000米，否则山体会倒塌。事实上，世界第一高峰——珠穆朗玛峰也不到9000米高。

简单的数学常识告诉我们，随着物体线度的增加，表面积将按平方数增加，而体积则按立方数增加。如果把燕子一模一样放大10倍，它们将再不能飞舞自如；老鼠如果增大10倍，从高楼上跌下来便再不会安然无恙(yàng)；而假如真有巨人，我们就算他们比普通人高大10倍吧，其体重将达到80吨，即正常人的1000倍，于是这可怜的巨人便会被自身体重压得寸步难行。

看看现实生活中的巨人那行动迟缓的样子，便会明白高大的体态使人类行动的灵活、敏捷大打折扣了。

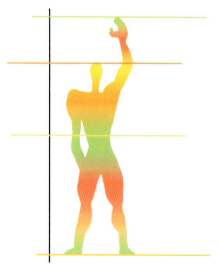

问题还远远不止于此。我们知道，长颈鹿需要用260厘米水银柱高的血压才能把血液送到头部，身材高大的人也需要较高的血压和更坚韧(rèn)的血管才能避免脑供血不足。而且，同时增加的负担还包括消化系统、呼吸系统和其他系统。

身材高大引起的生理上的困难还可以一直列举下去。统计数字指出，寿星老人大多是身材矮小的人。中国湖北省88名百岁老人的平均身高为143厘米，体重38公斤，调查报告把"瘦小的体形"列为长寿的第一要素。

再看一看周围的亲戚和朋友便不难发现，人类的身材正不断增高。近百年来，全球人类的平均身高直线上升。这种代代高的现象正引起各国政府和学者的注意。

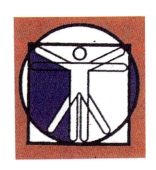

许多科学家对这一现象作出解答：营养的充足，医疗条件的改善，人类流动的增加，特别是远距离人群婚姻的增多……究竟什么才是人类身高不断增长的真正原因，还要进一步探索和证实。

而地球生命史上其他物种的兴(xīng)亡引起人类对自身命运的严肃思考。古生物学家告诉我们，恐龙的祖先原本都是小个子，经过亿万年，个头不断增大，终于变成生命史上最庞大的动物而走上末路。今日世界上的大象、长颈鹿、大熊猫，当初都曾有灵活小巧的身躯(qū)，随着一代代的变大，渐渐成为珍稀动物。可见身体增大不利于物种的生存和繁衍。人类难道不该从中引起警觉吗？

现在让我们把目光转向社会实际，看看人类身高增长会带来怎样的一连串问题。首先，民以食为天，根据计算，人类身高平均增长30厘米，便会多耗去50%的食物。而衣服面料的消耗也将惊人地增长。如果人的双脚大1/3，光一个美国，每年制作的皮鞋就要多用掉10,000平方千米的皮革。而在消耗的另一端，是废料的增加和污染。

还有，人是一切的尺度，尺度变了，一切都要变。日渐高大

的人类将对以前的生活环境感到不舒适：房屋低矮了，家具短小了，车船的客舱狭小了，生产工具不合手了。近来，美国许多古老戏院的座位，已容不下身材高大的年轻一代，而不得不重新装修。法国一家航空公司因乘客体重增大而减少收入。医生们则考虑是否必须加大药片的分量。很难设想某一天，人类会像换掉小了的衣服一样，换掉我们现存的无数文明成果。

人类是能够控制自己的唯一物种。应该改变我们对身高增长听其自然，甚至人为加速的危险做法了。富有远见的科学家、哲学家、政治家、社会学家和未来学家应该合作，求出人类最佳身材的解。

有位著名的经济学家说过："人是小的，小是美丽的，追求庞大，就是自杀。"至少我们要重新认真思考，在未来的地球上，我们应该成为什么样的人类。

（根据赵致真《我们应该长多高》改编）

生词

kūn chóng 昆虫	insect		qīn qi 亲戚	relative
guī dìng 规定	regulate		yī liáo 医疗	medical
jí ní sī 吉尼斯	Guinness		hūn yīn 婚姻	marriage
kǎo lǜ 考虑	consider		yán sù 严肃	serious
dòu fu 豆腐	tofu; bean curd		páng dà 庞大	enormous; huge
qiáo 瞧	look		fán yǎn 繁衍	procreate
wú xiàn 无限	infinitely; unlimitedly		jǐng jué 警觉	alertness
jì suàn 计算	calculate		xiāo hào 消耗	consume
fǒu zé 否则	otherwise		pí gé 皮革	leather
dūn 吨	ton		wū rǎn 污染	pollute
zhé kòu 折扣	discount		xiá xiǎo 狭小	narrow and small
xì tǒng 系统	system		zuì jiā 最佳	best

听写

灵活　吨　计算　庞大　婚姻　亲戚　污染

舒适　否则　考虑　＊瞧　最佳

比一比

繁 { 繁殖 / 繁衍 } 警 { 警察 / 警觉 } 舒 { 舒服 / 舒适 }

寿 { 寿星 / 长寿 } 规 { 规定 / 规矩 } 统 { 统计 / 系统 }

字词运用

亲戚

我在美国只有表姐一个亲戚。

我的亲戚大多数在中国。

污染

工业的发展造成了环境污染。

自然环境被污染了,有些地方下起了酸(suān)雨。

消耗

美国人每年要消耗大量的汽油。

运动可以消耗身上的脂肪(fáng)。

考虑　过滤

请让我考虑一下夏天去不去黄石公园。

自来水是经过过滤的水，比较干净。

否则

一到中国马上给妈妈打电话报平安，否则她会着急。

要看这部电影马上就得去，否则就晚了。

近义词

身躯——身体　　舒适——舒服　　瞧——看

至少——最少　　倒塌——垮

反义词

不利——有利　　　　狭小——宽大

词语解释

常识——普通的知识。

安然无恙——平平安安，没有出任何事故。

灵活——敏捷；善于随情况而改变；活动自如。

坚韧——牢固，即使受外力弯曲变形也不易破碎、折断。

充足——足够多，能满足需要。

改善——改进，使情况比原来更好。

废料——没有用的东西，废物。

汉语数字的表达

2.27 米 —— 二点二七米　　　3.8 公斤 —— 三点八公斤

50% —— 百分之五十　　　　0.48 米 —— 零点四八米

1000 倍 —— 一千倍　　　　　1/3 —— 三分之一

思考题

1. 人类身高的不断增长很危险吗？

2. 人类一代比一代高，是否会造成环境污染？

Lesson Nine

How High Should We Grow

Nature creates human beings, who are short in comparison with whales or elephants yet big in comparison with insects or mice. Human beings exists in the world within the size range regulated by nature.

The height of most men and women among the total population of several billion on the earth varies from 1.5 to 2 meters; a 2.27-meter American man and a 0.48-meter Dutch woman authorized by Guinness Book of Record are probably the tallest and the shortest human beings in the world so far.

People tend to believe that being tall means being healthy, strong, powerful and handsome. Yet do we ever think about the problem of how high should we grow? Firstly, let's talk about something that might seem irrelevant to broaden our thoughts. Here is a piece of ordinary bean curd, which maintains a good shape. Then if we make it bigger and bigger, what will happen to it? Yes, it will collapse. This experiment seems to be against tall people; is it that the weak strength of bean curd results in it and the experiment doesn't illustrate anything meaningful?

Then we can take the rock as another example. Can a rock mountain grow infinitely? According to relevant calculations, it is impossible for a mountain to exceed eleven kilometers in height; otherwise, the mountain will collapse. In fact, Mount Qomolangma (also known as the Everest), the highest in the world, doesn't reach 9 kilometers in height.

According to simple mathematic knowledge, as for an object, the increase of its dimension will result in a quadratic increase of its surface area and cubic increase of its size. A swallow that is ten times as large as an ordinary one cannot fly any more, a mouse that is ten times larger will no longer be safe falling down from a high building. If there is really giants on the earth and suppose they are ten times higher than ordinary man, then their weight will reach 80 metric tons and one thousand times heavier than ordinary man. Therefore, the poor giants will be too heavy for their legs to carry due to their own weight.

If you have ever noticed the slowness of real giants in moving and action, you will realize their massive size impairs their original flexibility and dexterity.

But this is not the whole story. As we know, a giraffe needs 260-mercury blood pressure to send its blood up to its brain; similarly, a tall man needs higher blood pressure and tougher blood vessels so as to avoid insufficient blood supply to brain. In addition, this also add burden to digestive system, respiratory system, and all other systems.

This list of biological difficulties caused by the taller body can go on and on. According to statistics, most long lived men and women are short people and the average height of 88 one-hundred-year-old people in Hubei Province is 143 centimeters, their average weight is 38 kilograms; therefore, the investigation report lists "slim and short figure" as the top element for longevity.

If you examine your relatives and friends, you will find that the height of mankind is increasing. According to statistics, during past one hundred years, the average height of global population has increased considerably and the phenomenon attracts the attention of both governments and scholars in all countries.

Some scientists manage to provide explanations to it: the sufficient nutrition, the improvement of medical conditions, the increase of human migration, and especially the increase of marriage between groups that used to be far apart. It requires further exploration and verification of the real reason behind the continuous growth of human beings.

Human beings should take serious consideration of their own fate referring to the rising and declining of other species in the history. Paleontologists prove that the ancestors of dinosaurs used to be short and through billions of years, evolution and growth, they grew continuously, became the largest creature in the history and are extinct at last. Elephants, giraffes and pandas used to have small and flexible bodies; after generations of growth, they became rare species today. It is obvious that the growth of body size goes against survival and reproduction of creatures and why shouldn't we learn lesson from the declining and extinction of many species?

Now let's turn our eyes to social reality and see a series of problems brought by the growth of man's height. Firstly, food is top priority of people and according to calculation, people consume 50% more food for an average growth of 30 centimeter. The consumption of fabric for clothing also increases considerably; if our feet are one third larger, in the US alone, 10,000 square kilometers more leather will be used every year to make leather shoes. The other side of consumption growth is the increase of wastes and pollution.

More profound consequence lies in the fact that people is the basic measurement for everything; its change will result in changes of almost everything. Increasingly tall human beings will no longer feel comfortable in the living environment created by our fathers and grandfathers. Houses will be too low, furniture will be too short, the space in both vehicles and boats will be too narrow and the production tools will no longer fit our hands. In recent years, the seats of many age-old theaters in US that are too small for tall young generation had to be reconstructed. The income of a French airline decreased due to the increase of passengers' weight. Doctors seriously consider increasing the dosage of medicine. It is hard to imagine that one day mankind will change our current numerous civilization fruits just as we change our short clothes that are no longer fit.

Human being is the only species that has power to control; we should change our original attitude of doing nothing to our body height growth, especially dangerous practice of accelerate our own growth. Scientists, philosophers, statesmen, economists and futurologists with vision should cooperate in finding the best solution concerning body height.

A famous economist once said: "Human being is small and to be small is beautiful, while to seek bulkiness is to commit suicide." We should at least think about it carefully: on the earth, what kind of human being are we going to be in the future.

Adapted from How High Shall We Grow by Zhao Zhihen

第十课

沙 漠

梁国宁

在茫茫宇宙中有一颗星，它是至今人类所知道的唯一有生命的星球。远远望去，它像一颗晶莹的蓝宝石。这就是人类的母亲——地球。

从卫星上看，地球并非这么完美，上面有几块黄色的斑点，这就是沙漠。说起沙漠，人们会有一种荒凉、恐惧的感觉。因为这里不像地球上其他地方那么湿润、美丽、生机盎然。这里缺少生命，干旱少雨，气候恶劣。阳光下，沙漠的气温可高达华氏一百三十几度（在死谷曾有华氏190度的高温）；而夜里，温度会下降到华氏二十几度，寒冷刺骨。如果刮起风来，飞沙走石，不见天日。一把生锈的刀，用不了多久就会被沙粒打磨得闪闪发光。很显然，这样的环境，人类是根本无法生存的。在地球上，沙漠大概占了陆地面积的20%。世界著名的沙漠有：非洲的撒哈拉沙漠，澳大利亚的维多利亚沙漠，西亚的阿拉伯沙漠，中国的塔克拉玛干沙漠、毛乌素沙漠以及戈壁沙漠等等。

沙漠形成的原因可以分成两种：自然原因和人为因素。由

于地球自转，在南北回归线附近形成了干热下沉的气流。在这种干燥季风的不断吹蚀（shí）下，形成了大面积的沙漠。在这一地带，白天、夜晚温差很大。岩石不断热胀冷缩，表面就会开裂、破碎，再被古代的冰川冲刷、堆积，就形成了"年轻的沙漠"——戈壁。戈壁的碎石再进一步风化，其中一些细小的颗粒被风刮走，又与其他石头摩擦，最后无数的石头小颗粒留在低洼的地区，形成了沙漠。在大风的作用下，一堆堆的沙子会形成巨大的沙丘，它还会慢慢地移动。在沙漠里，你会看到沙丘像一望无际的黄色的海洋。

自从有了人类，尤其是近代以来，人类进行的大规模的发展、建设，形成了所谓的"人造沙漠"，使沙漠的形成又多了一个人为的因素。由于世界人口增长过快，为了解决人类衣食住行的问题，不少地区乱砍滥伐，过度放牧，使大片森林遭到破坏，大片草原退化、沙化，水土不断流失。大批城市的出现，更使地球大气温度上升，沙漠化速度大大加快。还有，从古到今几千年，人类大大小小的战争从来没有停止过，每次战争都破坏了大量植被和绿

沙漠太阳能发电装置

地。仅第二次世界大战，各国烧毁的森林面积就有三个法国那么大。人类的活动成了当今地球沙漠化的重要原因。据联合国的报告，目前世界上每年都有近6万平方千米的土地沦为沙漠。

中国是一个沙漠面积比较大的国家。在960万平方千米的国土上，有约170万平方千米的沙漠。这些沙漠主要分布在西北地区，比如新疆、青海、内蒙古、甘肃、宁夏等省区，形成了一条长达万里的风沙危害线。每年都有十几次沙尘暴，威胁着中国1/3的国土，而且这种状况正在加重。据估计，沙漠的面积正以每年2000平方千米的速度在扩大着。古代

坎儿井

繁茂的森林不见了，昔日的绿洲——楼兰古国也被无情的黄沙吞没了。黄土高原曾经是草木茂盛的绿野，古代还有大象、老虎出没，如今则因严重的水土流失、干旱、沙化，而沦为中国最贫穷的地区之一。中国目前的生态环境真是令人担忧。

然而在浩瀚(hàn)的沙漠面前，人类真的束手无策、无所作为了吗？不是的，勤劳的、有智慧的人类，在改造沙漠方面，一直就有悠久的历史传统。中国在秦汉两代就修建了秦渠、汉渠，引黄河水来灌溉北方干旱的土地。在新疆沙漠地区，开凿了举世闻名的"坎儿井"，灌溉沙漠里的农田，使沙漠变成了绿洲。仅吐(tǔ)

鲁番地区的坎儿井就有数千千米。在包兰线铁路两侧，人们编草网格来固定沙丘。1978年以来，中国开始建设防护林工程，整个计划七十年完成。到时候将有一条长7000千米、宽400～1200千米的"绿色长城"在中国北方成长起来。在中东，人们用海水淡化装置生产淡水，来灌溉菜园、花园。为了减少水分蒸发，还建设了地下水库。在以色列，人们采用了电脑控制的滴灌技术。在美国，人们在沙漠中建起了像拉斯韦加斯这样著名的旅游城市。沙漠开始向人类低头了。

最近，随着科学家们的深入研究，人们发现沙漠下面埋着丰富的石油、天然气和多种矿藏。另外，沙漠独特的自然景观也可以发展沙漠旅游。沙漠多风少雨，阳光充足，是开发太阳能发电和风力发电的好地方。沙漠有待开发的地下水和光能，它又是生物人工养殖的好场所。用不尽的沙子是工业建设的天然材料……总之，沙漠是可以治理的，也是可以被合理利用的。

生词

jīng yíng 晶莹	sparkling and crystal-clear	dà pī 大批	many
bān diǎn 斑点	dot	jǐn jǐn 仅（仅）	only
kǒng jù 恐惧	fearful	lún wéi 沦为	be driven to
shēng xiù 生锈	rust	gū jì 估计	estimate
chì dào 赤道	equator	fán mào 繁茂	lush
huí guī xiàn 回归线	tropic	pín qióng 贫穷	poor
rè zhàng lěng suō 热胀冷缩	expand while hot, contract when cold	zhì huì 智慧	intelligence; wisdom
		yōu jiǔ 悠久	long in time
mó cā 摩擦	rub; friction	chuán tǒng 传统	tradition
dī wā 低洼	low-lying	kǎnr jǐng 坎儿井	Kerez well
yóu qí 尤其	particularly	zhuāng zhì 装置	device
suǒ wèi 所谓	so-called	shuǐ kù 水库	reservoir

听写

尤其　　恐惧　　仅仅　　大批　　生锈　　勤劳　　智慧

传统　　贫穷　　水库　　*热胀冷缩

比一比

摩（摩擦）　　尤（尤其）　　及｛以及　　繁｛繁茂
磨（磨刀）　　由（由于）　　　　及格　　　　繁殖

贫（贫穷）　　估（估计）　　统｛传统　　湿｛湿润
贪（贪心）　　古（古代）　　　　系统　　　　潮湿

洼（低洼）　　锈（生锈）　　库｛水库　　束｛束手无策
娃（娃娃）　　绣（绣花）　　　　车库　　　　结束

字词运用

尤其

我喜欢图画，尤其喜欢国画。

小明体育好，尤其是篮球打得好。

仅（仅）

范浩学得真快，他仅仅用了十几分钟，就把这几个生词全学会了。

以及

院子里种着瓜果蔬菜以及鲜花。

他到过北京、上海、广州以及重庆等城市。

近义词

恐惧——害怕　　繁茂——茂盛　　利用——使用

反义词

湿润——干燥　　　　　贫——富

大批——少量　　　　　胀——缩

多音字

cáng
藏

zàng
藏

cáng 藏 { 矿藏 / 躲藏 }

zàng 藏 { 宝藏 / 西藏 }

tǔ   tù
吐   吐
tǔ   tù
吐鲁番   上吐下泻

sā   sǎ
撒   撒
sā   sǎ
撒哈拉沙漠   撒了

词语解释

荒凉——人烟稀少；冷清。

生机盎然——形容到处是一片充满生命力的样子。

浩瀚——形容广大、一望无际。

束手无策——比喻像捆住了手，没有办法。

无所作为——不努力做出成绩，或者没有做出成绩。

举世闻名——在全世界都有名。

相配词语连线

效果　　　　　利用

污染　　　　　增加

解决　　　　　良好

合理　　　　　环境

数量　　　　　问题

阅读

坎儿井

到吐鲁番旅游，你可以看见绿洲旁边的戈壁滩上，顺高坡而下，有一堆一堆的圆土包，远看就像穿成串的珍珠伸向绿洲，这就是坎儿井。到了吐鲁番，一定要看坎儿井。坎儿井是吐鲁番的水源，没有坎儿井，就没有吐鲁番绿洲，也就没有吐鲁番的葡萄。

坎儿井并不是一口井，而是一条人工挖出的地下河。为什么要在地下挖河呢？这是因为吐鲁番盆地四周是高山和沙漠，气候干燥、炎热，水分蒸发很快，风沙又大，地面水渠常被黄沙淹埋；而坎儿井是地下河流，不受风沙和炎热天气的影响，可以

常年灌溉农田。新疆大约有坎儿井1600多条，其中在吐鲁番就有1200多条，总长超过5000千米。

坎儿井的水源在哪儿呢？吐鲁番虽然干旱少雨，但是盆地的北方有天山山脉，夏季有大量冰川融水流向盆地，渗入戈壁，提供了丰富的水源。于是当地的居民就把高山雪水作为水源，再利用山的坡度挖地下河，引水灌溉良田。

坎儿井是由竖井、地下水渠、地面水渠、涝坝（水池）四部分组成的。坎儿井的地下水渠并不是我们想象中的地沟，而是可供人出入的地道，不过在地道中间有一条水渠。吐鲁番地区土质坚实，挖好的地道不易垮塌。地下河的出口与地面水渠相连接，以便灌溉田地。用不完的水可以存放在涝坝里。

坎儿井是一种结构巧妙的地下水利工程。它的历史很久远。吐鲁番现存的坎儿井多为清朝所建，如今坎儿井的清泉仍旧灌溉着吐鲁番的大地，维持着戈壁绿洲的一片生机。这里生产的葡萄、哈密瓜和棉花名扬中外。坎儿井与万里长城、京杭大运河并称为中国古代三大工程。

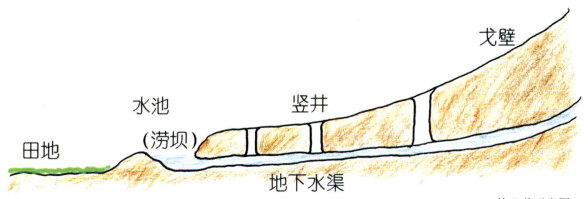

坎儿井示意图

Lesson Ten

The Desert

There is a star in vast universe and it's the only planet known to mankind as the one blessed with living creatures. From far distance, it looks like a crystal sapphire and this is our mother planet, the earth.

Viewed from satellites, however, the earth is far from being perfect, for there are several yellowish dots on it and these are deserts. The word of desert will inevitably remind people of a desolate and dreaded feeling, for the place is no moist, beautiful and lively as other places on the earth. There are seldom plants and creatures here, for the place suffers drought, little rain and bad climate. Under the sunshine, the temperature here will reach over 130 degrees Fahrenheit (the temperature at the Dead Valley is even higher at 190 degrees). But during the night, the temperature will drop sharply to a freezing 22 degrees Fahrenheit. When wind blows, flying sand and moving rocks will blind the sky and a rusty knife will soon become shining bright polished by the sand. It is obvious that human being can't survive the environment here. The deserts account for about 20% of the entire land area on earth and the famous deserts include the Sahara Desert in Africa, the Victoria Desert of Australia, the Arabian Desert in West Asia, the Taklamakan Desert, the Mu Us Desert and the Gobi Desert in China, etc.

The reasons to form the deserts fall into two main categories: natural reasons and man-made reasons. Due to the rotation of the earth, xerothermic and down draft has been formed near both Tropic of Cancer and Tropic of Capricorn and a large area of desert exists due to the continuous corrosion of dry monsoon. In these areas, the temperature difference of day and night is huge, resulting in a continuous expansion and shrink due to heat, accordingly the surface of rocks here will crack and break up, creating "young desert-Gobi" through erosion and accumulation by ancient glaciers. With the impact of further aeolation, the fine articles of broken rocks will be blown by the wind and rub with other rocks, resulting in the accumulation of numerous rock particles in low areas, and this is desert. Driven by strong wind, piles of sand will form gigantic sand dunes moving slowly forward. In desert, you will see vast yellow sea of sand dunes.

After human beings came to the picture and especially after the large scale development and construction in modern times, the "man-made deserts" appear, creating another source for the formation of desert. Due to fast growth of population in the world, in order to tackle with various issues including clothing, food, residence, and transport, a lot of areas have been overly developed by cutting forests, raising stocks and a large area of forests has been destroyed, the plains suffer desertification, resulting in a continuous soil erosion. The construction of more and more cities makes the temperature go up and accelerates the process of desertification. Moreover, during several thousand years from the ancient time, wars of different scales never stop among people and each one of them destroyed a large amount of plantation and green land. Taking the World War Two as an example, the total area of forests burned in

different countries equaled to three France. Human activities serve as the main reason of current desertification and according to a report released by the UN, nearly 60,000 square kilometers land becomes desert each year in the world.

The area of deserts in China is relatively large, for among a total territory of 9.6 million square kilometers, 1.7 million is deserts, most of which are located in the northwest area covering Xinjiang, Qinghai, Inner Mongolia, Gansu, and Ningxia, creating a dangerous sandstorm line with a total length of 10,000 li. Every year, a dozen of sandstorms threaten one third of Chinese territory and the situation becomes increasingly worse. It is estimated that the desert area increases by 2,000 square kilometers each year. The flourishing ancient forests have gone, taking away with them the ancient oasis; the Ancient Loulan State has been buried under the yellow sand. The Loess Plateau used to be flourishing with grass and trees and a green paradise for elephants and tigers. But today, due to severe soil erosion, drought, and desertification, it becomes one of the most poverty-stricken areas in China. More and more people become concerned about the ecological environment in China.

In front of the vast deserts, is it real that we can do nothing about it? The answer is No, for industrious and intelligent human beings have always devoted in transforming deserts. During both dynasties of Qin and Han, ancient Chinese built the Qin Canal and the Han Canal to divert water from the Yellow River in irrigating the land in dry north area. The desert area of Xinjiang is famous for its unique irrigation system of Kerez wells that can change desert into oasis. The total length of Kerez wells reach several thousand meters in Turpan area alone. Along both sides of Baotou-Lanzhou Railway, local people make hay grid to fix sand dunes. Since 1978, China has dedicated to the planting of protection forests and plans to accomplish the project in 70 years. At that time, there will be a Green Great Wall 7,000 km long and 400-1,200 km wide in North China. In the Middle East, people use desalinating units to produce fresh water for irrigating vegetable land and gardens. In order to reduce evaporation, they also build underground reservoirs. In Israel, computer-controlled dropping irrigation technology has been adopted; in the US, people build world famous tourist cities such as Las Vegas in desert. In front of mankind, deserts begin to lower their heads.

Recently, along with the deepening of scientific research, people discover abundant oil, natural gas and mineral resources under deserts. Moreover, the unique natural view also makes deserts become attractive tourist destinations. Since deserts feature little rain yet sufficient wind and solar power, they are the best places for developing solar and wind electricity power. The undeveloped underground water and light energy also makes it an ideal place for raising live stocks and its inexhaustible sand resource can be used as the natural material for industrial construction. In a word, when it comes to desert, there is a way out and there are reasonable solutions.

The Kerez Well

When you travel in Turpan area, you will see piles of rounded mounts located along high banks in Gobi close to the oasis. Standing at a distance, they look like stringed pearls extending to the oasis and they are Kerez wells, places you don't want to miss when you visit Turpan. These wells are water sources in the area; without them, there will be no Turpan oasis and no delicious Turpan grapes.

In fact, the Kerez well is not actually a well; instead, it is a man-made underground stream. Why do the local people dig a river under the ground? Because the Turpan Basin is surrounded by high mountains and deserts, the climate here is dry and hot, therefore water evaporates quickly. Moreover, the strong wind storm brings yellow sand and will bury ground canals. Since Kerez wells are located underground and not affected by both wind storm and hot weather, they can be used to irrigate farming land all year long. There are more than 1,600 Kerez wells in Xinjiang, among which over 1,200 are located in Turpan alone and the total length is more than 5,000 kilometers.

Then where is the water source for these wells? Although the place suffers drought and little rain, there is Tianshan Mountain to the north of the basin and during summer, a large amount of water melt from snow and ice will flow into the basin and under the ground of Gobi area, serving as abundant water source for the area. The local people will find water source from snow mountains and then dig underground stream along the mountain slope to irrigate farming land.

A Kerez well is composed of four parts of shaft well, underground ditch, ground canal, and water pool. The underground ditch is not the usual trench we are familiar with but tunnels that people can walk through, and there is a canal in the middle of the tunnel. The soil of Turban area is solid and therefore the tunnel won't collapse. The exit of the underground stream connects with the ground canal irrigating farming land and the unused water can be stored in the pool.

The Kerez well is a cleverly-designed underground water conservancy system with a long history. Most of the existing Kerez wells in Turpan were built during the Qing Dynasty and are still used to irrigate the farming land in the area, maintaining the lively Gobi oasis. The grapes, melons, fruits and cotton produced in this area are popular in both domestic and international markets; and the Kerez well, the Great Wall, the Beijing-Hangzhou Grand Canal are famed as three leading projects handed down from ancient China.

生字表(简)

1. 究(jiū) 某(mǒu) 喷(pēn) 坦(tǎn) 程(chéng) 宗(zōng) 咚(dōng) 雅(yǎ) 泽(zé) 屹(yì) 碑(bēi) 则(zé) 谜(mí)

2. 涓(juān) 汇(huì) 鄂(è) 倍(bèi) 雁(yàn) 挤(jǐ) 粪(fèn) 鳞(lín) 钓(diào)

3. 抖(dǒu) 异(yì) 繁(fán) 殖(zhí) 仁(rén) 掘(jué) 溪(xī) 孑(jié)

4. 蘑(mó) 菇(gū) 秒(miǎo) 概(gài) 迅(xùn) 刹(shā) 控(kòng) 膝(xī) 炮(pào)

5. 骆(luò) 驼(tuó) 饲(sì) 畜(chù) 驯(xùn) 境(jìng) 劣(liè) 栖(qī) 摄(shè) 补(bǔ) 迁(qiān) 徙(xǐ) 胁(xié) 暴(bào) 舒(shū)

   翼(yì) 腔(qiāng) 酷(kù) 范(fàn) 祸(huò)

6. 恒(héng) 纬(wěi) 甚(shèn) 超(chāo) 掠(lüè) 腾(téng)

7. 倦(juàn) 厘(lí) 凝(níng) 屑(xiè) 蒸(zhēng) 囱(cōng) 毁(huǐ) 废(fèi) 肺(fèi) 铅(qiān) 罩(zhào) 洒(sǎ)

8. 盐(yán) 汲(jí) 塌(tā) 窟(kū) 窿(lóng) 捆(kǔn) 竿(gān) 哗(huā) 熬(áo) 滤(lǜ) 熄(xī) 搅(jiǎo) 获(huò)

9. 尼(ní) 斯(sī) 虑(lǜ) 腐(fǔ) 瞧(qiáo) 限(xiàn) 否(fǒu) 吨(dūn) 扣(kòu) 统(tǒng) 戚(qī) 疗(liáo) 姻(yīn) 庞(páng)

   衍(yǎn) 警(jǐng) 耗(hào) 革(gé) 污(wū) 染(rǎn) 狭(xiá) 佳(jiā)

10. 莹(yíng) 惧(jù) 锈(xiù) 摩(mó) 洼(wā) 尤(yóu) 谓(wèi) 批(pī) 仅(jǐn) 沦(lún) 估(gū) 茂(mào) 贫(pín) 慧(huì) 悠(yōu)

    坎(kǎn) 库(kù)

共计 129 个生字

生字表（繁）

1. 究(jiū) 某(mǒu) 噴(pēn) 坦(tǎn) 程(chéng) 宗(zōng) 咚(dōng) 雅(yǎ) 澤(zé) 屹(yì) 碑(bēi) 則(zé) 謎(mí)

2. 涓(juān) 匯(huì) 鄂(è) 倍(bèi) 雁(yàn) 擠(jǐ) 糞(fèn) 鱗(lín) 釣(diào)

3. 抖(dǒu) 異(yì) 繁(fán) 殖(zhí) 仁(rén) 掘(jué) 溪(xī) 孑(jié)

4. 蘑(mó) 菇(gū) 秒(miǎo) 概(gài) 迅(xùn) 刹(shā) 控(kòng) 膝(xī) 炮(pào)

5. 駱(luò) 駝(tuó) 飼(sì) 畜(chù) 馴(xùn) 境(jìng) 劣(liè) 棲(qī) 攝(shè) 補(bǔ) 遷(qiān) 徙(xǐ) 脅(xié) 暴(bào) 舒(shū) 翼(yì) 腔(qiāng) 酷(kù) 範(fàn) 禍(huò)

6. 恒(héng) 緯(wěi) 甚(shèn) 超(chāo) 掠(lüè) 騰(téng)

7. 倦(juàn) 厘(lí) 凝(níng) 屑(xiè) 蒸(zhēng) 囪(cōng) 毀(huǐ) 廢(fèi) 肺(fèi) 鉛(qiān) 罩(zhào) 灑(sǎ)

8. 鹽(yán) 汲(jí) 塌(tā) 窟(kū) 窿(lóng) 捆(kǔn) 竿(gān) 嘩(huā) 熬(áo) 濾(lù) 熄(xī) 攪(jiǎo) 獲(huò)

9. 尼(ní) 斯(sī) 慮(lù) 腐(fǔ) 瞧(qiáo) 限(xiàn) 否(fǒu) 噸(dūn) 扣(kòu) 統(tǒng) 戚(qī) 療(liáo) 姻(yīn) 龐(páng)

   衍(yǎn) 警(jǐng) 耗(hào) 革(gé) 污(wū) 染(rǎn) 狹(xiá) 佳(jiā)

10. 瑩(yíng) 懼(jù) 銹(xiù) 摩(mó) 窪(wā) 尤(yóu) 謂(wèi) 批(pī) 僅(jǐn) 淪(lún) 估(gū) 茂(mào) 貧(pín) 慧(huì) 悠(yōu)

    坎(kǎn) 庫(kù)

共計 129 個生字

生词表(简)

1. 究竟 证实 考察 某地 喷泉 阿勒坦郭勒 路程
   约古宗列 叮咚 雅拉达泽 屹立 石碑 原则
   谜(语) 挥手

2. 涓涓 汇(合) 鄂陵湖 两倍 把…弄浑 倒映 大雁
   拥挤 粪 鳞(片) 钓鱼

3. 抖动 恐龙 衰亡 雌雄异株 繁殖 乔木 果仁
   可惜 进化 地质 演化 古雅 避难所 挖掘 溪
   孑遗植物

4. 运动员 降落 迟缓 表演 蘑菇 紧张 熟练
   技巧 公式 秒 阻力 大概 迅速 刹车 控制
   膝盖 炮 掌握

5. 骆驼 饲养 家畜 状态 驯化 环境 恶劣 栖息地
   摄氏 适应 补充 交配 迁徙 威胁 风暴 舒服
   鼻翼 鼻腔 严酷 禁止 范围 天灾人祸

6. 恒星 持久 卫星 火箭 精密 仪器 经度 纬度
   现象 甚至 超过 物体 关系 一掠而过 慢腾腾
   视线

7. 灰尘 疲倦 晴朗 显微镜 厘米 凝结 作用 碎屑
   蒸发 粉末 烟囱 毁坏 废品 肺炎 金属 铅
   口罩 事故 防止 洒水 利益 服务

8. 盐 区别 露天 汲水 倒塌 圆圈 窟窿 直径 捆
   竹竿 哗哗 熬 影响 过滤 熄灭 搅动 获得
   能干

9. 昆虫 规定 吉尼斯 考虑 豆腐 瞧 无限 计算
   否则 吨 折扣 系统 亲戚 医疗 婚姻 严肃 庞大
   繁衍 警觉 消耗 皮革 污染 狭小 最佳

10. 晶莹 斑点 恐惧 生锈 赤道 回归线 热胀冷缩
    摩擦 低洼 尤其 所谓 大批 仅（仅） 沦为
    估计 繁茂 贫穷 智慧 悠久 传统 坎儿井
    装置 水库

共计 185 个生词

生詞表（繁）

1. 究竟 證實 考察 某 噴泉 阿勒坦郭勒 路程 約古宗列 叮咚 雅拉達澤 屹立 石碑 原則 謎（語） 揮手

2. 涓涓 匯（合） 鄂陵湖 兩倍 把…弄渾 倒映 大雁 擁擠 糞 鱗（片） 釣魚

3. 抖動 恐龍 衰亡 雌雄異株 繁殖 喬木 果仁 可惜 進化 地質 演化 古雅 避難所 挖掘 溪 孑遺植物

4. 運動員 降落 遲緩 表演 蘑菇 緊張 熟練 技巧 公式 秒 阻力 大概 迅速 剎車 控制 膝蓋 炮 掌握

5. 駱駝 飼養 家畜 狀態 馴化 環境 惡劣 棲息地 攝氏 適應 補充 交配 遷徙 威脅 風暴 舒服 鼻翼 鼻腔 嚴酷 禁止 範圍 天災人禍

6. 恒星（héng xīng） 持久（chí jiǔ） 衛星（wèi xīng） 火箭（huǒ jiàn） 精密（jīng mì） 儀器（yí qì） 經度（jīng dù） 緯度（wěi dù） 現象（xiàn xiàng） 甚至（shèn zhì） 超過（chāo guò） 物體（wù tǐ） 關係（guān xì） 一掠而過（yí lüè ér guò） 慢騰騰（màn tēng tēng） 視綫（shì xiàn）

7. 灰塵（huī chén） 疲倦（pí juàn） 晴朗（qíng lǎng） 顯微鏡（xiǎn wēi jìng） 厘米（lí mǐ） 凝結（níng jié） 作用（zuò yòng） 碎屑（suì xiè） 蒸發（zhēng fā） 粉末（fěn mò） 烟囪（yāncong） 毀壞（huǐ huài） 廢品（fèi pǐn） 肺炎（fèi yán） 金屬（jīn shǔ） 鉛（qiān） 口罩（kǒuzhào） 事故（shì gù） 防止（fǎng zhǐ） 灑水（sǎ shuǐ） 利益（lì yì） 服務（fú wù）

8. 鹽（yán） 區別（qū bié） 露天（lù tiān） 汲水（jí shuǐ） 倒塌（dǎo tā） 圓圈（yuán quān） 窟窿（kū long） 直徑（zhí jìng） 捆（kǔn） 竹竿（zhú gān） 嘩嘩（huāhuā） 熬（áo） 影響（yǐng xiǎng） 過濾（guò lǜ） 熄滅（xī miè） 攪動（jiǎo dòng） 獲得（huò dé） 能幹（néng gàn）

9. 昆蟲（kūn chóng） 規定（guī dìng） 吉尼斯（jí ní sī） 考慮（kǎo lǜ） 豆腐（dòu fu） 瞧（qiáo） 無限（wú xiàn） 計算（jì suàn） 否則（fǒu zé） 噸（dūn） 折扣（zhé kòu） 系統（xì tǒng） 親戚（qīn qi） 醫療（yī liáo） 婚姻（hūn yīn） 嚴肅（yán sù） 龐大（páng dà） 繁衍（fán yǎn） 警覺（jǐng jué） 消耗（xiāo hào） 皮革（pí gé） 污染（wū rǎn） 狹小（xiá xiǎo） 最佳（zuì jiā）

10. 晶瑩（jīng yíng） 斑點（bāndiǎn） 恐懼（kǒng jù） 生銹（shēng xiù） 赤道（chì dào） 回歸綫（huí guī xiàn） 熱脹冷縮（rè zhàng lěng suō） 摩擦（mó cā） 低窪（dī wā） 尤其（yóu qí） 所謂（suǒ wèi） 大批（dà pī） 僅（僅）（jǐn） 淪爲（lún wéi） 估計（gū jì） 繁茂（fán mào） 貧窮（pín qióng） 智慧（zhì huì） 悠久（yōu jiǔ） 傳統（chuán tǒng） 坎兒井（kǎnr jǐng） 裝置（zhuāng zhì） 水庫（shuǐ kù）

共計 185 個生詞

第一课

一 写生词

究	竟										
某	地										
喷	泉										
坦											
路	程										
宗											
叮	咚										
屹	立										
石	碑										
原	则										
谜	语										
雅	拉	达	泽								

二 组词

喷_____   谜_____   坦_____   屹_____

究_____   某_____   则_____   证_____

察_____   碑_____   挥_____   咚_____

三 选字组词

(源 原)头　　　路(成 程)　　　(吃 屹)立

(挥 辉)手　　　(证 正)明　　　(谜 迷)语

四 写出反义词

弯曲——　　　有——　　　窄——

安静——　　　长——　　　高——

干净——　　　乱——　　　忘——

五 选择填空

1. 黄河流过中国的_____。（南方　北方）

2. 唐代诗人李白曾在诗中写道："_____之水天上来"。

（长江　黄河）

3. 2000多年前,汉朝的_____向汉武帝报告,黄河水是从塔里木河流来的。(张骞 李春)

4. _____政府派出了第一个河源考察队。

(元朝 汉朝)

5. 1952年,中国的河源考察队断定_____为黄河的正源。(卡日曲 约古宗列曲)

6. 一块刻着"黄河源"三个大字和一行藏文的石碑立在_____河边。(卡日曲 约古宗列曲)

7. 后来人们从卫星照片上发现了卡日曲比约古宗列曲还要长_____千米。(一百二十五 二十五)

8. 卡日曲应该是_____正源。(黄河的 长江的)

9. 清朝政府一共派出了_____河源考察队。

(两个 一个)

六 造句

1. 表示_____

2. 究竟_____

3. 兴奋_____

七 根据阅读材料选择填空

1. 巴音布鲁克的天鹅湖位于中国_____。

（青海　新疆）

2. 天鹅湖在_____。（高山上　盆地里）

3. 天鹅湖的水是_____的雪水融化而来的。

（天山　长白山）

4. 湖泊四周有许多_____。（海子　清泉）

5. 每到_____,在印度和非洲南部过冬天的天鹅都要飞回这里。（秋季　春季）

八 根据阅读材料判断对错

1. 湖上的天鹅成千上万。　　　　　　　　___对　___错

2. 天鹅在湖边草丛(cóng)里做窝生蛋。　　___对　___错

3. 小天鹅出壳三四个小时就能游水找食。___对　___错

4. 一个月的功夫,小天鹅便可长到10公斤重。　　　　　　　　　　　　　　　___对　___错

5. 巴音布鲁克天鹅湖是自然保护区。　　___对　___错

九 缩写《黄河的源头(一)》(300字左右)

十 朗读课文

第三课

一 写生词

抖	动										
繁	殖										
果	仁										
挖	掘										
溪											
雌	雄	异	株								
子	遗	植	物								

二 组词

仁_____   折_____   抖_____   绝_____

衰_____   俗_____   雌_____   雄_____

异_____ 溪_____ 殖_____ 乔_____

雅_____ 迹_____ 避_____ 掘_____

三 选词填空

骄傲　　娇气　　大桥　　乔木

1. 金门_____在旧金山。

2. 银杏是落叶_____。

3. 虚心使人进步，_____使人落后。

4. 小妹妹一点也不_____，摔倒了，自己爬起来。

四 根据课文判断对错

1. 银杏是中国特有的古老树种。　　___对　___错

2. 银杏是长得又高又大的落叶乔木。　　___对　___错

3. 银杏的叶子像一把小折扇。　　___对　___错

4. 银杏树足足有两亿多年的历史。　　___对　___错

5. 银杏树与恐龙一块儿生活过。　　___对　___错

6. 科学家们叫松树为"活化石"。　　___对　___错

7. 银杏有个俗名叫"公孙树"。　　___对　___错

8. 银杏是一种生长很慢的树木。　　　　　___对　___错

9. 银杏是雌雄同株的。　　　　　　　　　___对　___错

10. 银杏的果仁也是一种药。　　　　　　 ___对　___错

11. 水杉是珍贵而又稀有的植物。　　　　 ___对　___错

12. 水杉是一种秀丽而古雅的树木。　　　 ___对　___错

13. 只有中国还有水杉,在别的国家它早已绝种了。　　　　　　　　　　　　 ___对　___错

14. 1941年,中国有一位教授在广东发现了水杉。　　　　　　　　　　　　 ___对　___错

五 造句

1. 诞生_____

2. 逐渐_____

六 根据课文回答问题

1. 水杉是怎样被发现的?

答:_____

_____

2. 为什么银杏是研究生物进化、地质演化、古代气候的难得材料？（选做题）

答：_____

七 根据阅读材料判断对错

1. 有一种草是长在虫子身上的。　　　　　___对　___错

2. 冬虫夏草上边是根草，下边是条虫子。　___对　___错

3. 只有在夏天，冻（dòng）土刚刚融化的时候，才能在山上找到冬虫夏草。　　　　　___对　___错

4. 冬虫夏草是一种菌类，像蘑菇一样，自己能制造养料。　　　　　　　　　　　___对　___错

5. 冬虫夏草自己长大了，可是虫子却被它吸干了。　　　　　　　　　　　　　___对　___错

6. 冬天时，这是一条虫子，而到了夏天，虫子身上却长出了像草似的菌丝，这就是冬虫夏草。　　＿＿对　＿＿错

八　请写一写"冬虫夏草"的名字是怎么来的

_____

_____

_____

_____

_____

九　朗读课文

第五课

一 写生词

骆	驼										
饲	养										
家	畜										
驯	化										
环	境										
恶	劣										
栖	息	地									
摄	氏										
补	充										
迁	徙										
威	胁										
风	暴										

舒	服											
鼻	翼											
鼻	腔											
严	酷											
范	围											
天	灾	人	祸									

二 组词

骆_____ 态_____ 饲_____ 畜_____

暴_____ 概_____ 存_____ 境_____

补_____ 胁_____ 禁_____ 岁_____

邮_____ 票_____ 范_____ 舒_____

三 写出反义词

准许——　　　　　　　　　难受——

四 给多音字注音

1. 图书馆里禁（　　）止大声说话。

2. 小妹妹着急了，禁（　　）不住哭了起来。

五 选词填空

补充　　威胁　　禁止　　舒服

1. 核武器_____着世界和平。

2. 小弟弟讲故事讲得不完全，小妹妹又_____了几句。

3. 医院里_____吸烟。

4. 这个座位很窄小，小胖坐着不_____。

六 根据课文判断对错

1. 中国新疆阿尔金山一带有野骆驼生活。　___对　___错

2. 中国的野骆驼是双峰驼。　　　　　　　___对　___错

3. 仅有一小部分双峰驼处于野生状态。　　___对　___错

4. 在中国生存的野生双峰驼为原生的野生种。　　　___对　___错

5. 早在中国的汉代,就有了关于骆驼的记载。　　　___对　___错

6. 明朝李时珍的《本草纲目》中也提到了野骆驼。　　　___对　___错

7. 科学家在罗布泊考察时见到了野骆驼。___对　___错

8. 野骆驼吃的是几乎没有叶子的植物,喝的是盐水。　　　___对　___错

9. 野骆驼在不喝一滴水的情况下,在炎热的沙漠上能行走两个星期。　　　___对　___错

10. 有水的时候,野骆驼一下子能喝下多达200千克的水。　　　___对　___错

11. 野骆驼越来越少,目前已经不到1000只了。　　　___对　___错

七 造句

　　本领_____

八 词语解释

　　1. 荒凉——

　　2. 剧烈——

九 根据课文回答问题

　　为什么人是野骆驼的最大威胁？

　　答：_____

　　_____

　　_____

　　_____

　　_____

十 朗读课文

第七课

一 写生词

疲	倦											
厘	米											
凝	结											
碎	屑											
蒸	发											
烟	囱											
毁	坏											
废	品											
肺	炎											
铅												
口	罩											
洒	水											

二 组词

尘_____ 倦_____ 者_____ 郊_____

朗_____ 舞_____ 洒_____ 微_____

镜_____ 燥_____ 宅_____ 铅_____

毁_____ 康_____ 防_____ 废_____

三 选择填空

1. 晚上小华用_____观察天空中的星星。

（显微镜　望远镜）

2. 在实验室里学生们正用_____观察细菌。

（镜子　显微镜　望远镜）

3. 在大城市的住宅区里，空气中的灰尘比_____多。

（郊野　剧院）

4. 空气很干_____。（燥　躁 zào）

5. 天气_____朗。（晴　睛）

6. 酒瓶子摔碎了，酒_____了一地。（洒　撒）

四 根据课文判断对错

1. 小的灰尘比细菌还小,用显微镜也看不到。　　　___对　___错

2. 在城市住宅区的空气里,灰尘要比野外少得多。　　　___对　___错

3. 灰尘会帮助空气中的水分凝结成云雾和雨点。　　　___对　___错

4. 没有灰尘,就没有白云,也没有大雨和小雨了。　　　___对　___错

5. 灰尘能使气温降低。　　　___对　___错

6. 有机的灰尘有花粉、棉絮、种子等。　　　___对　___错

7. 灰尘落到机器里,会使机器的光滑部分磨坏。　　　___对　___错

8. 灰尘里面还有病菌和病毒,会让人生病。　　　___对　___错

9. 粉尘还会引起爆炸。　　　___对　___错

10. 石灰和水泥的灰尘,会损害我们的肺
    和皮肤。　　　　　　　　　　　___对　___错

11. 每一个工厂都应该有通风设备和吸
    尘设备。　　　　　　　　　　　___对　___错

五 根据课文回答问题

1. 天然的灰尘是从哪里来的?

   答:_____

   _____

   _____

   _____

2. 人工的灰尘是从哪里来的?

   答:_____

   _____

   _____

   _____

六 根据阅读材料判断对错

1. 空气中并不是总含着水。　　　　　　　　＿＿对　＿＿错

2. 你看不到空气中的水,也感觉不出空
   气中有水。　　　　　　　　　　　　　　＿＿对　＿＿错

3. 雾就是水蒸气。　　　　　　　　　　　　＿＿对　＿＿错

4. 雾是无数细的水滴。　　　　　　　　　　＿＿对　＿＿错

5. 天气闷热的时候,汗水也停止了蒸发。　　＿＿对　＿＿错

6. 云是由细微的水滴组成的。　　　　　　　＿＿对　＿＿错

7. 靠近地面的空气总比较热,含的水
   蒸气也比较多。　　　　　　　　　　　　＿＿对　＿＿错

8. 空中的雾就是云。　　　　　　　　　　　＿＿对　＿＿错

9. 有的云不是由水滴,而是由细小的冰
   晶组成的。　　　　　　　　　　　　　　＿＿对　＿＿错

10. 卷云很高,飞得很快,几乎跟飞机
    一样快。　　　　　　　　　　　　　　＿＿对　＿＿错

11. 积云成为雷云,一场大雷雨就快来了。　＿＿对　＿＿错

12. 6000米厚的云变成雨,落到地上的雨水还不到10毫米。　　___对　___错

七　朗读课文

第九课

一 写生词

吉	尼	斯									
考	虑										
豆	腐										
瞧											
无	限										
否	则										
吨											
折	扣										
系	统										
亲	戚										
医	疗										
婚	姻										

庞大
繁衍
警觉
消耗
皮革
污染
狭小
最佳

二 组词

统_____ 警_____ 昆_____ 虑_____

姻_____ 肃_____ 革_____ 庞_____

价_____ 戚_____ 否_____ 耗_____

计_____ 污_____ 佳_____ 疗_____

三 写出近义词

舒适——　　　　至少——　　　　瞧——

四 写出反义词

　　有利——　　　　　狭小——　　　　　敏捷——

五 选择填空

　　1. 地球上几十亿人身高的_____是从一米五到两米。

（周围　范围）

　　2. 人们往往认为,高大_____着健康和俊美。

（味道　意味）

　　3. 医疗条件的_____是人类身高增长的原因之一。

（改变　改善）

　　4. 恐龙的_____原本都是小个子。（祖先　爷爷）

　　5. 石头山不能够_____增高。（有限　无限）

　　6. 美国一家航空公司因乘客体重增大而_____收入。

（减少　减小）

六 选词填空

　　　　折扣　　污染　　灵活　　亲戚

　　1. 每年春节前,商店都卖打_____的商品。

2. 有的地区经济虽然发展很快，但是自然环境被严重_____。

3. 在体操比赛中，小双的动作不但难度大，而且_____、_____、优美。

4. 姑姑是我的_____。

七 根据课文判断对错

1. 豆腐做得太大就会垮。　　　　　　　　　___对　___错

2. 人类身高增长会带来许多问题。　　　　　___对　___错

3. 在地球上，山的高度不能超过十千米。　　___对　___错

4. 如果老鼠增大10倍，从高楼上跌下来便
   可能摔死。　　　　　　　　　　　　　___对　___错

5. 巨人会被自身体重压得寸步难行。　　　　___对　___错

6. 身材高大的人需要较低的血压。　　　　　___对　___错

7. 长寿老人常是身材高大的人。　　　　　　___对　___错

8. 人类的身材正在不断增高。　　　　　　　___对　___错

八 造句

    1. 充足_____

    2. 否则_____

    3. 考虑_____

九 词语解释

    1. 安然无恙(yàng)——

    2. 改善——

    3. 常识——

十 回答问题

1. 你认为人类身高的不断增加对人类是好事还是坏事？为什么？

    答：_____

_____

_____

_____

2. 人类一代比一代高对环境会造成什么影响？举例说明。

答：_____

_____

_____

_____

十一 朗读课文

第一课听写

第三课听写

第五课听写

第七课听写

第九课听写

第二课

一 写生词

涓	涓										
汇	合										
鄂	陵	湖									
两	倍										
大	雁										
拥	挤										
粪											
鳞	片										
钓	鱼										

二 组词

汇_____ 涛_____ 镜_____ 倍_____

浑_____ 映_____ 雁_____ 挤_____

粪_____ 捕_____ 钓_____ 缓_____

三 选词填空

把……弄浑　　整齐　　挥手　　拥挤　　成群结队

1. 请不要_____水_____！

2. 火车开动了,爸爸从车窗口向我_____告别。

3. 放学了,学生们_____地走出校门。

4. 作业要写得干净_____。

5. 上海南京路的商店里人来人往,十分_____。

四 根据课文填空

鄂陵湖的水深差不多是扎陵湖的两_____。湖水的颜色总是_____的。站在湖边,一眼望不到边的湖水,随风而起的阵阵_____,你一定以为到了_____的大海了。每当风和日丽,湖水平静的时候,四周白色的雪山,天空飘浮的白云,全都_____在蓝色的湖面上,就像_____美丽的图画。

五 根据课文判断对错

1. 黄河从发源地的细流汇成一条河流后，首先流进了星宿海。　　___对　___错

2. 星宿海是个四周是山地的积水盆地。　　___对　___错

3. 星宿海里散布着数不清的大大小小的"海子"。　　___对　___错

4. 黄河在星宿海里散乱地流过，没有正式的河道。　　___对　___错

5. 扎陵湖是咸水湖。　　___对　___错

6. 扎陵湖和鄂陵湖也是黄河流域内的两个最大的湖泊。　　___对　___错

7. 扎陵湖水的颜色总是蓝蓝的。　　___对　___错

8. 鄂陵湖比扎陵湖大，水也深。　　___对　___错

9. 每当天气好的时候，扎陵湖和鄂陵湖看上去就像美丽的图画。　　___对　___错

10. 鄂陵湖湖心有鸟岛，6月前后，地上到处
    是成堆的鸟蛋。　　　　　　　　　　___对　___错

11. 岛上的水鸟大都是捕鱼的能手。　　　___对　___错

12. 湖水中的鱼也不少，都是有鳞片的高原
    冷水鱼。　　　　　　　　　　　　　___对　___错

13. 高原湖水中的鱼，一点也不怕冷，生
    长也很快。　　　　　　　　　　　　___对　___错

14. 高原湖区的鱼一点也不怕人。　　　　___对　___错

15. 在这里捕鱼或钓鱼可太容易了。　　　___对　___错

六　造句

1. 倍_____

2. 拥挤_____

3. 除了……以外_____

   _____

七 根据课文回答问题

1. "星宿海"这个美丽的名字是怎样得来的？

答：_____

_____

_____

_____

2. 扎陵湖在藏语中是什么意思？

答：_____

_____

3. 鄂陵湖在藏语中是什么意思？

答：_____

_____

八 词语解释

1. 人烟稀少——

2. 成稀结队——

九 朗读课文

第四课

一 写生词

蘑	菇											
秒												
大	概											
迅	速											
刹	车											
控	制											
膝	盖											
炮												

二 组词

降_____ 缓_____ 演_____ 蘑_____

巧_____ 刹_____ 阻_____ 抵_____

增_____ 膝_____ 盖_____ 炮_____

伍_____　　散_____　　枪_____　　掌_____

迅_____　　概_____　　控_____　　运_____

三 选字组词

（炮　跑）兵　　　公（试　式）　　　（衣　依）靠

（炮　跑）步　　　考（试　式）　　　（衣　依）裳

依（辈　靠）　　　（刹　杀）车　　　大（既　概）

一（辈　靠）子　　（刹　杀）死　　　（既　概）然

四 选词填空

底下　　低头　　抵消　　增加　　曾经

1. 树_____站着的那个人好像是个警察。

2. 她_____看了看手表。

3. 这两种药不能同时吃，不然药的效力就_____了。

4. 在当总统之前他_____当过律师。

5. 世界人口不断_____。

五 选择填空

1. 因为下大雨,有的同学_____了。(迟到 迟早)

2. 打篮球有许多_____。(技巧 技术)

3. 没多久,他就_____了开车的技术。(掌握 手掌)

4. 春节的时候小朋友们很喜欢放_____。

(书包 花炮)

六 根据课文判断对错

1. 跳伞运动员只需要体格健壮、技术熟练。

___对 ___错

2. 有的运动员能在离地面20米的时候才打开降落伞。

___对 ___错

3. 从2000米的高空,运动员跳出飞机降落到地面,前后用不了五分钟。

___对 ___错

4. 我们乘火车和汽车时,要是车开得很快的时候猛一刹车,身体就会向前冲去。

___对 ___错

5. 跳伞快到地面时两条腿并好,屈起膝
   盖。这样落地时,腿不会受伤。　　___对　___错

6. 伞兵常采用"迟缓跳伞"的技术躲开敌
   人炮火的射击。　　　　　　　　___对　___错

七 造句

1. 大概_____
2. 尽量_____
3. 紧张_____

八 词语解释

1. 技巧——
2. 并非如此——

九 朗读下面的句子两遍

1. 百川东到海,何时复西归?

   少壮不努力,老大徒伤悲!

2. 时间如流水,一去不复返。

3. 一寸光阴一寸金,寸金难买寸光阴。

4. 我们爱惜时间,就像爱惜自己的生命。

十 根据阅读材料,请谈一谈自己对"时间就是生命"的看法

_____

_____

_____

_____

_____

十一 朗读课文

第六课

一 写生词

恒	星									

纬	度									

甚	至									

超	过									

慢	腾	腾								

一	掠	而	过							

二 组词

测_____　　纬_____　　掠_____　　系_____

腾_____　　视_____　　仪_____　　持_____

甚_____　　精_____　　超_____　　恒_____

三 写出反义词

静止—— 　　　　　固定——

四 根据课文判断对错

1. 恒星是动的。　　　　　　　　　　　　___对　___错

2. 恒星运动的速度比宇宙火箭快好几倍。___对　___错

3. 其实星座的形状也在变。　　　　　　　___对　___错

4. 中国古代天文学家一行生活在8世纪初。　　　　　　　　　　　　　　　　　___对　___错

5. 一行和几个人一起制造了黄道浑仪,用来测量星宿的经纬度。　　　　　　　___对　___错

6. 一行发现恒星的经度、纬度都在变。　　___对　___错

五 造句

1. 甚至_____

2. 超过_____

六 根据课文回答问题

为什么我们看不出恒星是动的呢？（请至少写五句话）

答：_____

_____

_____

_____

_____

七 相配词语连线

扩大　　　　　环境

有趣的　　　　范围

保护　　　　　故事

熟练的　　　　矿藏

坚强的　　　　变化

剧烈的　　　　技巧

开采　　　　　意志

八 根据阅读材料判断对错

1. 飞上天空的宇航员看到的地球,是一个晶莹明亮的球体,周围有一层薄薄的水蓝色"纱衣"。　　＿＿对　＿＿错

2. 地球是生命的摇篮,是人类的母亲。　　＿＿对　＿＿错

3. 地球在茫茫宇宙中是一个不大的星球。　　＿＿对　＿＿错

4. 人类生活的陆地大约只占地球面积的1/5。

　　＿＿对　＿＿错

5. 地球的自然资源是无限(xiàn)的,用也用不完。

　　＿＿对　＿＿错

6. 地球矿产资源是经过百万年,甚至几亿年的地质变化才形成的。　　＿＿对　＿＿错

7. 人类不应该无计划地乱开采资源。　　＿＿对　＿＿错

8. 人类生活所需要的水资源、森林资源、生物资源、大气资源本来是可以不断再生的。　　　　___对　___错

9. 我们要精心地保护地球,保护地球的生态环境。　　　　　　　　___对　___错

九 根据阅读材料回答问题

我们为什么要精心地保护地球?

答:_____

_____

_____

_____

_____

十 朗读课文

第八课

一 写生词

盐											
汲 水											
倒 塌											
窟 窿											
捆											
竹 竿											
哗 哗											
熬											
过 滤											
熄 灭											
搅 动											
获 得											

二 组词

含_____ 澡_____ 影_____ 砖_____

圈_____ 经_____ 挡_____ 盐_____

获_____ 钩_____ 桶_____ 滤_____

锅_____ 搅_____ 捆_____ 能_____

三 选字组词

(钢 刚)铁　　　饭(锅 祸)　　　铁(沟 钩)

(钢 刚)才　　　车(锅 祸)　　　水(沟 钩)

四 写出近义词

牢固——　　　凭——　　　扎——

五 给多音字注音

老鼠钻(　　)进洞里了。

钻(　　)机正在钻(　　)一口油井。

今年的狂欢节盛(　　　)况空前。

拿这个碗盛(　　　)米饭。

六 选词填空

露天　　砖头　　窟窿　　直径　　水桶　　影响

1. 水井大多数是_____的。

2. 这个盘子的_____是八寸。

3. 盐井里汲水的_____是用长竹竿做的。

4. 明明发现毛衣上有许多虫子咬的小_____。

5. 上课乱说话会_____别人听课。

6. 不知是谁扔了一块_____,差一点打着我的头。

七 根据课文判断对错

1. 盐井里的水是咸的,里面含有盐。　　　___对　___错

2. 盐井的井口只有汤盆口大小,但是有近千米深。　　　___对　___错

3. 千米深的盐井,全是人工凿成的。　　　___对　___错

4. 在 2350 年以前,四川已经开凿盐井了。

              ___对 ___错

5. 打盐井用的绳子,是一片片的竹片连起来

 做成的绳子。   ___对 ___错

6. 水桶是用打通了节的粗竹竿连起来做

 成的。   ___对 ___错

7. 井盐是把盐水放在锅里熬出来的。 ___对 ___错

8. 下雨天也可以照样开采井盐。 ___对 ___错

9. 每个水井上都有个高高的木架子。 ___对 ___错

10. 从井里汲起来的盐水很干净。 ___对 ___错

八 造句

1. 影响_____

2. 能干_____

九 根据阅读材料判断对错

1. 电影的生日是 1895 年 2 月 8 日。 ___对 ___错

2. 法国巴黎的许多报社记者、剧院经理、科学家和社会名流,来到大咖啡馆的地下室。　　＿＿对　＿＿错

3. 由于人们从来没看过电影,闹了许多笑话。　　＿＿对　＿＿错

4. 自从有了电影之后,人们非常喜欢看电影。　　＿＿对　＿＿错

十 请写一写人们第一次看电影闹了哪些笑话

_____

_____

_____

_____

_____

十一 朗读课文

第十课

一 写生词

晶	莹										
恐	惧										
生	锈										
摩	擦										
低	洼										
尤	其										
所	谓										
大	批										
仅	仅										
沦	为										
估	计										
繁	茂										

贫	穷									
智	慧									
悠	久									
坎	儿	井								
水	库									

二 组词

锈_____ 侧_____ 斑_____ 胀_____

茂_____ 估_____ 勤_____ 智_____

悠_____ 库_____ 装_____ 仅_____

洼_____ 尤_____ 贫_____ 批_____

三 选字组词

(磨 摩)擦　　大(批 比)　　生(绣 锈)

(磨 摩)刀　　(批 比)较　　(绣 锈)花

(尤 由)于　　传(统 充)　　以(级 及)

(尤 由)其　　(统 充)足　　年(级 及)

四 反义词连线

湿润　　　　　很少

大量　　　　　富

贫　　　　　　干燥

五 根据课文判断对错

1. 在宇宙中,月球是唯一有生命的星球。　___对　___错

2. 在地球上,沙漠大概占了陆地面积的 20%。　___对　___错

3. 沙漠形成的原因分为自然原因和人为因素两种。　___对　___错

4. 目前世界上每年都有大片土地沦为沙漠。　___对　___错

5. 中国沙漠面积较大,每年都有十几次沙尘暴。　___对　___错

6. 中国沙漠的面积正以每年2000平方
千米的速度在扩大。　　　　　　　　___对　___错

7. 古代的黄土高原曾经是草木茂盛的绿野。___对　___错

8. 中国北方已经开始建造"绿色长城"。___对　___错

9. 沙漠下面埋着丰富的石油、天然气和多
种矿藏。　　　　　　　　　　　　___对　___错

10. 沙漠是发展太阳能发电和风力发电的
好地方。　　　　　　　　　　　　___对　___错

六　词语解释

1. 举世闻名——

2. 束手无策——

3. 无所作为——

七　请写一写"人造沙漠"是怎么形成的（如：人口、砍树、放牧、城市、战争）

_____

_____

八 请写一写人类用什么办法改造沙漠

九 朗读课文

第二课听写

第四课听写

第六课听写

第八课听写

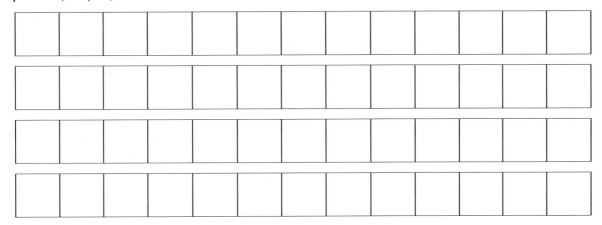

第十课听写

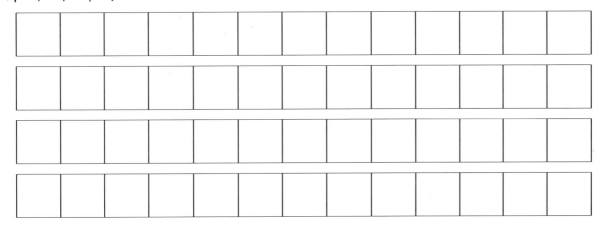